MathFlare

Name: ____________________________

Class: ___________

Teacher: ____________________________

Introduction

As parents and educators, we recognize the pivotal role mathematics plays in shaping a child's academic journey and future success. Yet, the path to mathematical proficiency can often seem daunting, fraught with challenges and complexities. That's where the transformative power of MathFlare Workbooks shine through, illuminating the way forward with clarity, precision, and purpose.

Introducing MathFlare Workbooks – a beacon of guidance, a testament to excellence, and a catalyst for achievement. Crafted with meticulous care and expertise, MathFlare Workbooks stand as paragons of educational excellence, designed to nurture young minds, ignite a passion for learning, and develop a deep-rooted understanding of mathematical concepts.

Picture this: your child eagerly delves into the pages of Mathflare Workbook, greeted by a step-by-step guide illuminated with vivid examples that demystify complex mathematical concepts. With each turn of the page, they embark on a journey of discovery, encountering thoughtfully curated practice questions that reinforce learning and hone problem-solving skills. And when they unveil the answers to those very questions, a sense of accomplishment blossoms within them – a tangible reward for their hard work and dedication.

But MathFlare Workbooks are more than just tools for learning; they are pathways to comprehension, fostering a deep-seated understanding of mathematical concepts through a sequential, logical flow. From fundamental principles to advanced problem-solving strategies, every chapter builds upon the last, ensuring a robust foundation upon which future knowledge can be constructed.

As parents, we yearn for nothing more than to see our children thrive, to witness the spark of inspiration ignited within them as they conquer academic challenges with confidence and poise. MathFlare Workbooks serve as partners in this noble endeavor, offering not just practice questions, but the keys to unlocking a world of opportunity.

And for teachers, MathFlare Workbooks stand as invaluable allies in the quest to cultivate mathematical proficiency in the classroom. With answers readily available, instructors can focus on guiding and nurturing their students, confident in the knowledge that MathFlare Workbooks provide a solid framework upon which to build.

In the pages of MathFlare Workbooks, we find not just the promise of academic excellence, but the seeds of a brighter tomorrow. So let us embrace the power of mathematics, let us champion the journey of learning, and let us pave the way for a generation of young minds poised to shape the world. With MathFlare Workbooks as our guide, the possibilities are infinite, and the future, bright.

Table of Contents

MathFlare
MATH WORKBOOK
2
Step by Step Guide and Essential Practice with Answers
Addition Subtraction
Multiplication
Place Value and Expanded Notations
Geometry

MathFlare
MATH WORKBOOK
2-3
Step by Step Guide and Essential Practice with Answers
Addition Subtraction
Multiplication and Division
Place Value and Expanded Notations
Geometry

MathFlare
MATH WORKBOOK
3
Step by Step Guide and Essential Practice with Answers
Multiplication and Division
Decimals
Place Value and Expanded Notations
Fractions and Geometry

MathFlare
MATH WORKBOOK
1
Step by Step Guide and Essential Practice with Answers
Counting and Numbers
Addition and Subtraction
Place Value and Expanded Notations
Understanding Time

MathFlare
MATH WORKBOOK
1-2
Step by Step Guide and Essential Practice with Answers
Counting and Numbers
Addition and Subtraction
Place Value and Expanded Notations
Understanding Time

MathFlare
MATH WORKBOOK
3-4
Step by Step Guide and Essential Practice with Answers
Addition Subtraction
Multiplication Division
Place Value and Expanded Notations
Fractions and Geometry

MathFlare
MATH WORKBOOK
4
Step by Step Guide and Essential Practice with Answers
Addition Subtraction
Multiplication Division
Place Value and Expanded Notations
Fractions and Geometry

MathFlare
MATH WORKBOOK
4-5
Step by Step Guide and Essential Practice with Answers
Multiplication Division
Place Value and Expanded Notations
Fractions and Geometry
Unit Conversion

MathFlare
MATH WORKBOOK
Grade 5
Step by Step Guide and Essential Practice with Answers
Multiplication Division
Place Value and Expanded Notations
Fractions and Geometry
Unit Conversion
MathFlare Publishing

MathFlare
MATH WORKBOOK
Grade 5-6
Step by Step Guide and Essential Practice with Answers
Multiplication Division
Place Value and Expanded Notations
Fractions and Geometry
Units and Statistics
MathFlare Publishing

MathFlare
MATH WORKBOOK
Grade 6
Step by Step Guide and Essential Practice with Answers
Integers and Statistics
Arithmetic and Pre-Algebra
Fractions and Geometry
Ratio and Percentage
MathFlare Publishing

MathFlare
MATH WORKBOOK
Grade 6-7
Step by Step Guide and Essential Practice with Answers
Arithmetic and Pre-Algebra
Ratio, Percent Proportion
Geometry
Statistics
MathFlare Publishing

MathFlare
MATH WORKBOOK
Grade 7
Step by Step Guide and Essential Practice with Answers
Pre-Algebra
Ratio, Percent Proportion
Geometry
Statistics
MathFlare Publishing

MathFlare
MATH WORKBOOK
Grade 7-8
Step by Step Guide and Essential Practice with Answers
Pre-Algebra
Ratio, Percent Proportion
Geometry and Cartesian Plane
Statistics
MathFlare Publishing

MathFlare
MATH WORKBOOK
Grade 8-9
Step by Step Guide and Essential Practice with Answers
Pre-Algebra
Ratio, Proportion and Percentage
Linear Equations
Geometry and Cartesian Plane
MathFlare Publishing

MathFlare
MATH WORKBOOK
Grade 8
Step by Step Guide and Essential Practice with Answers
Pre-Algebra
Percentage
Linear Equations
Geometry
MathFlare Publishing

Place Value and Expanded Notations

Place value tells us the value of a digit in a number based on where it's placed.

Imagine we have the number 647.528. It has 6 digits.

Now, each digit holds a special place. Let's break down the number 647.528:

- The digit 6 is in the hundreds place. Its value is 6×100=600.

- The digit 4 is in the tens place. Its value is 4×10=40.

- The digit 7 is in the ones place. Its value is 7×1=7.

- The digit 5 is in the tenths place. Its value is $5 \times \frac{1}{10} = 0.5$.

- The digit 2 is in the hundredths place. Its value is $2 \times \frac{1}{100} = 0.02$.

- The digit 8 is in the thousandths place. Its value is $8 \times \frac{1}{1000} = 0.008$.

When we add these values together, we find the value of the entire number:

$$600 + 40 + 7 + 0.5 + 0.02 + 0.008 = 647.528$$

Let's solve some problems:

Place value of the underlined digit:

600.5̲28 = __5 tenths__

Expanded notations:

891,479	800,000 + 90,000 + 1,000 + 400 + 70 + 9
691,905	6 hundred thousands + 9 ten thousands + 1 thousand + 9 hundreds + 5 ones
988.582	9 hundreds + 8 tens + 8 ones + 5 tenths + 8 hundredths + 2 thousandths

Rounding Numbers

Rounding numbers is the process of approximating a numerical value to a certain degree of accuracy by replacing it with a simpler or more convenient value. Rounding is commonly used to simplify calculations and express numbers in a more manageable form.

Steps to Rounding Numbers:

1. **Identify the digit to be rounded:** Determine the digit to which the number will be rounded.

2. **Look at the next digit:** Examine the digit immediately to the right of the one being rounded.

3. **Decide whether to round up or down:** If the next digit is 5 or greater, round the digit up. If it is less than 5, round the digit down.

4. **Adjust the number:** Change the digit being rounded and replace all digits to the right with zeros if necessary.

Properties of Rounding Numbers:

1. **Accuracy:** Rounding reduces the precision of a number but maintains its approximate value.

2. **Simplicity:** Rounding simplifies calculations by using fewer digits.

3. **Ease of Use:** Rounding makes numbers easier to work with, especially in mental arithmetic and estimation.

Methods of Rounding Numbers:

1. **Round to Nearest Integer:** Round to the nearest whole number.

    I.   Round Up (Ceiling): Always round up to the nearest integer.
    II. Round Down (Floor): Always round down to the nearest integer.

2. **Round to Nearest Tenth:** Round to the nearest tenth (one decimal place).

3. **Round to Nearest Hundredth:** Round to the nearest hundredth (two decimal places).

4. **Round to Nearest Thousandth:** Round to the nearest thousandth (three decimal places).

5. **Round to Specific Decimal Places:** Round to a specified number of decimal places as needed.

Let's round the number **438,576.214** to various degrees of accuracy:

Rounding Level	Rounded Number	Difference from Original
Nearest Whole Number	438,576	0
Nearest Ten	438,580	+4
Nearest Hundred	438,600	+24
Nearest Thousand	439,000	+424
Nearest Ten Thousand	440,000	+3,424
Nearest Hundred Thousand	400,000	−38,576
Nearest Million	0.4386×10^6	−438,576.214

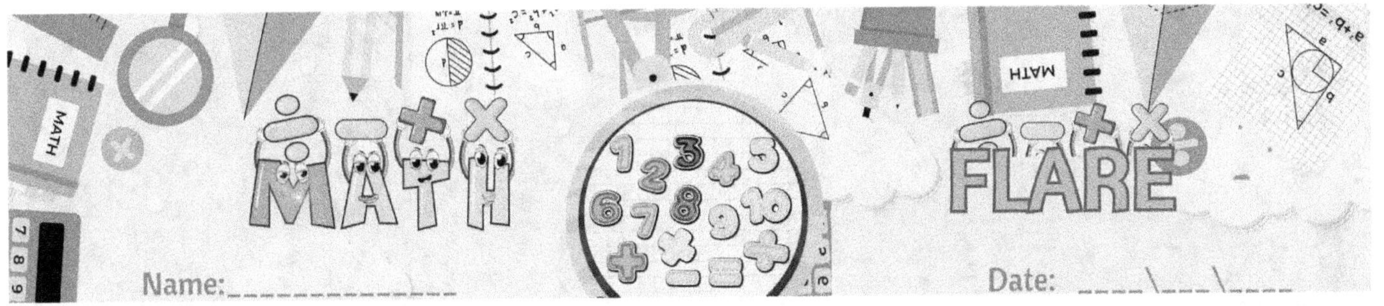

Place Value

Determine the place value of the underlined digit.

1. 9 6̲ 5.1 = _________________

2. 3 5̲ 3.32 = _________________

3. 56 7̲.15 = _________________

4. 5 9̲ 7.4 = _________________

5. 258.3 4̲ = _________________

6. 247.8 9̲ = _________________

7. 53 9̲.82 = _________________

8. 5̲ 08.75 = _________________

9. 2̲ 34.47 = _________________

10. 812. 2̲ = _________________

11. 99 1̲.43 = _________________

12. 173. 6̲ 9 = _________________

13. 3 0̲ 6.78 = _________________

14. 21 3̲.79 = _________________

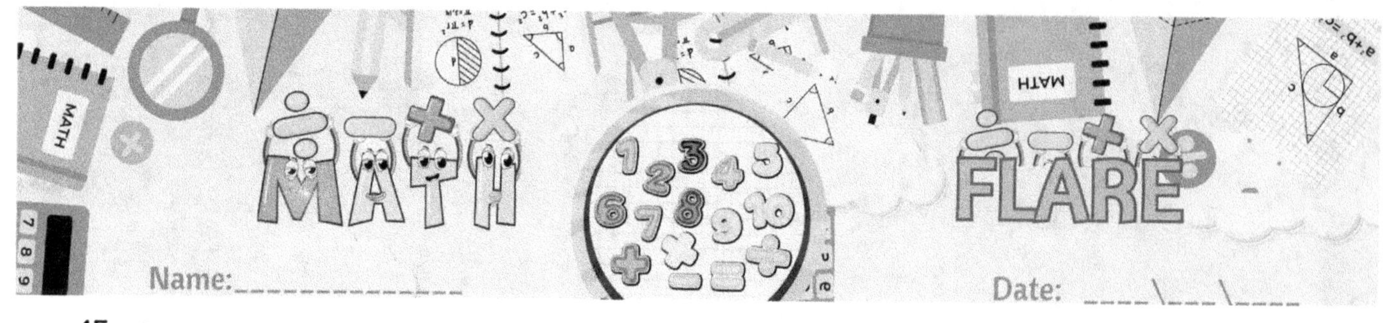

15. 291.1_3 = _______________

16. 612.1_2 = _______________

17. 3_7_3.54 = _______________

18. 5_0_7.26 = _______________

19. 65_8_.83 = _______________

20. 645._3_5 = _______________

21. _5_73.37 = _______________

22. 12_5_.85 = _______________

23. _6_16.44 = _______________

24. 48_3_.26 = _______________

25. _8_71.72 = _______________

26. 301._7_7 = _______________

27. 115._7_2 = _______________

28. _3_60.13 = _______________

29. _2_76.54 = _______________

30. 962.6_9_ = _______________

Name:________________________   Date: _______________

31. 392.32 = ________________   32. 340.01 = ________________

33. 799.22 = ________________   34. 308.74 = ________________

35. 229.99 = ________________   36. 870.43 = ________________

37. 553.42 = ________________   38. 818.5 = ________________

39. 366.94 = ________________   40. 852.58 = ________________

41. 790.86 = ________________   42. 388.7 = ________________

43. 296.12 = ________________   44. 404.58 = ________________

45. 224.8 = ________________   46. 154.34 = ________________

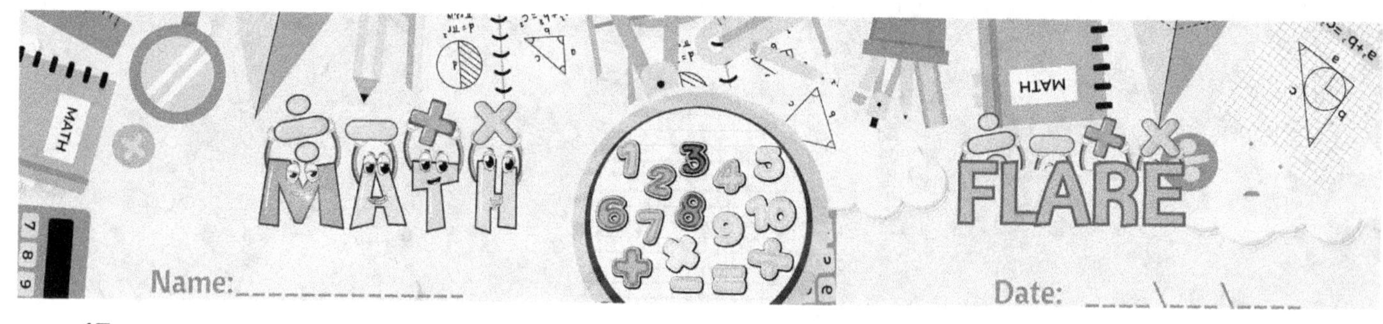

47. 508.7<u>6</u> = _______________

48. 716.9<u>7</u> = _______________

49. 170.0<u>8</u> = _______________

50. <u>8</u>55.16 = _______________

51. 346.3<u>1</u> = _______________

52. 804.<u>9</u>1 = _______________

53. 6<u>6</u>7.2 = _______________

54. 20<u>7</u>.24 = _______________

55. 216.<u>1</u>6 = _______________

56. <u>9</u>39.25 = _______________

57. 7<u>3</u>6.87 = _______________

58. <u>1</u>83.89 = _______________

59. 725.<u>6</u>7 = _______________

60. 956.<u>5</u>6 = _______________

61. 232.1<u>7</u> = _______________

62. <u>2</u>79.69 = _______________

Place Value: Expanded Notation

Provide the expanded notation for each value.

63. _________________ 3 hundreds + 8 tens + 2 ones + 2 tenths + 7 hundredths

64. _________________ 6 hundreds + 6 tens + 5 ones + 5 tenths + 5 hundredths

65. _________________ 5 hundreds + 4 tens + 6 tenths + 7 hundredths

66. _________________ 6 hundreds + 2 tens + 4 ones + 9 tenths

67. _________________ 9 hundreds + 2 tens + 5 ones + 1 tenth + 1 hundredth

68. _________________ 9 hundreds + 2 tens + 2 ones + 8 tenths + 1 hundredth

69. _________________ 8 hundreds + 1 ten + 1 one + 8 tenths + 5 hundredths

70. _________________ 4 hundreds + 3 tens + 9 ones + 2 tenths + 3 hundredths

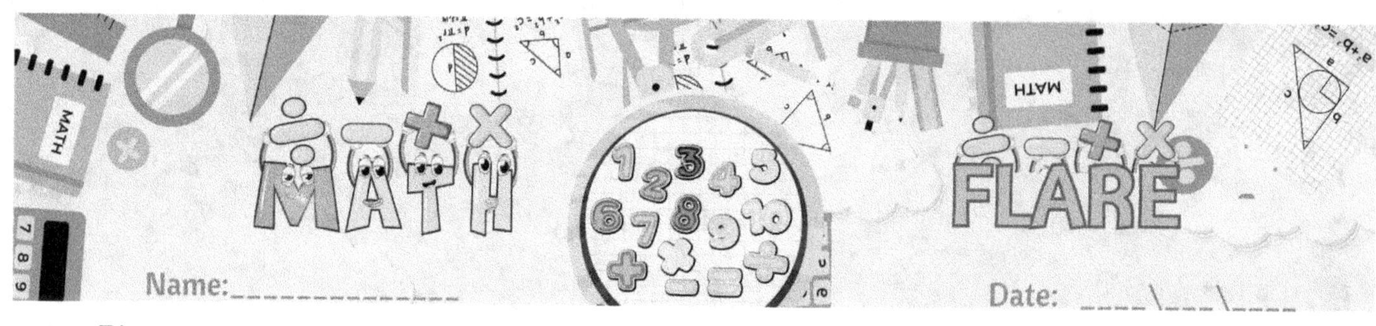

71. __________________ 2 hundreds + 6 tens + 1 one + 9 hundredths

72. __________________ 1 hundred + 8 tens + 1 one + 2 tenths + 1 hundredth

73. __________________ 7 hundreds + 8 ones + 5 tenths + 3 hundredths

74. __________________ 6 hundreds + 4 tens + 4 ones + 1 tenth + 1 hundredth

75. __________________ 2 hundreds + 8 tens + 4 ones + 5 tenths + 4 hundredths

76. __________________ 2 hundreds + 4 tens + 6 ones + 8 tenths + 1 hundredth

77. __________________ 8 hundreds + 8 tens + 6 ones + 9 tenths + 8 hundredths

78. __________________ 6 hundreds + 2 tens + 1 one + 5 tenths + 3 hundredths

79. __________________ 2 hundreds + 4 tens + 5 ones + 6 tenths + 5 hundredths

80. _______________ 5 hundreds + 6 tens + 8 ones + 9 tenths + 6 hundredths

81. _______________ 9 hundreds + 5 tens + 2 ones + 2 tenths + 3 hundredths

82. _______________ 3 hundreds + 9 tens + 4 ones + 7 tenths + 5 hundredths

83. _______________ 1 hundred + 9 tens + 7 ones + 4 tenths

84. _______________ 6 hundreds + 5 ones + 2 tenths + 7 hundredths

85. _______________ 9 hundreds + 4 tens + 1 tenth + 2 hundredths

86. _______________ 5 hundreds + 6 tens + 2 ones + 2 tenths + 3 hundredths

87. _______________ 2 hundreds + 7 ones + 3 tenths + 1 hundredth

88. _______________ 4 hundreds + 2 tens + 9 ones + 6 hundredths

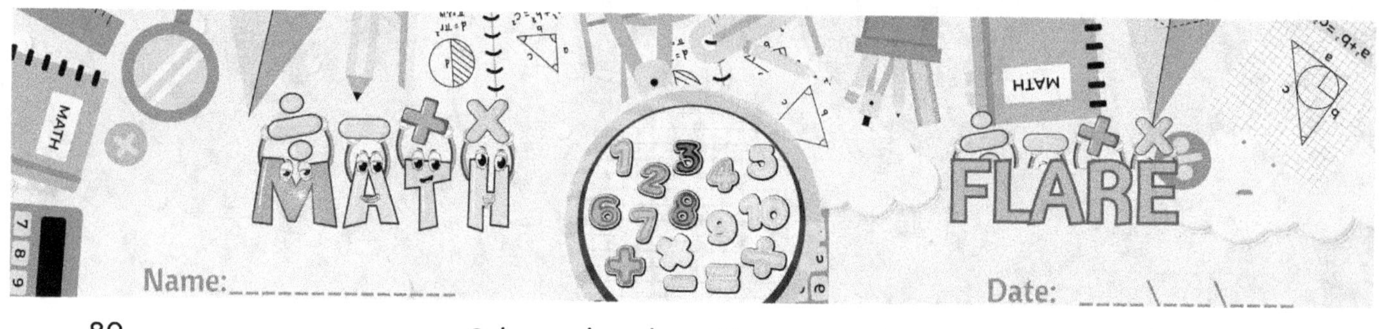

89. _________________ 8 hundreds + 3 tens + 4 ones + 6 tenths + 4 hundredths

90. _________________ 7 hundreds + 7 tens + 5 ones + 1 tenth + 1 hundredth

91. _________________ 1 hundred + 9 ones + 4 tenths + 4 hundredths

92. _________________ 8 hundreds + 3 ones + 3 tenths

93. _________________ 4 hundreds + 4 ones + 1 tenth + 5 hundredths

94. _________________ 1 hundred + 9 tens + 7 ones + 8 tenths + 5 hundredths

95. _________________ 9 hundreds + 4 tens + 3 tenths + 2 hundredths

96. _________________ 8 hundreds + 7 tens + 7 tenths + 7 hundredths

97. _________________ 8 hundreds + 8 tens + 1 one + 2 tenths + 9 hundredths

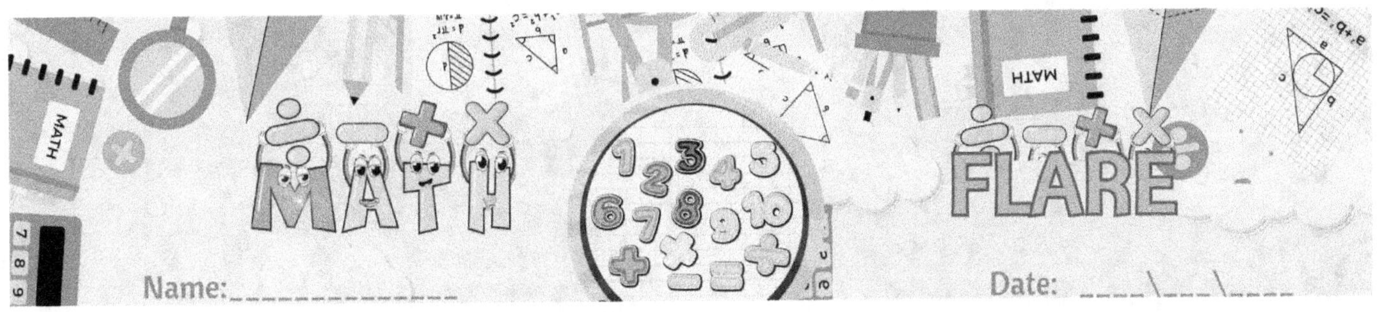

98. ___________ 2 hundreds + 6 tens + 7 ones + 8 tenths + 7 hundredths

99. ___________ 5 hundreds + 4 tens + 8 ones + 9 tenths + 6 hundredths

100. ___________ 3 hundreds + 8 tens + 5 ones + 9 tenths + 3 hundredths

101. ___________ 6 hundreds + 3 tens + 2 tenths + 6 hundredths

102. ___________ 1 hundred + 9 ones + 6 tenths + 5 hundredths

103. ___________ 3 hundreds + 6 tens + 6 ones + 7 tenths + 6 hundredths

104. ___________ 3 hundreds + 4 tens + 3 ones + 2 tenths + 4 hundredths

105. ___________ 7 hundreds + 4 tens + 4 ones + 3 tenths + 6 hundredths

106. ___________ 7 hundreds + 1 ten + 1 one + 8 tenths + 4 hundredths

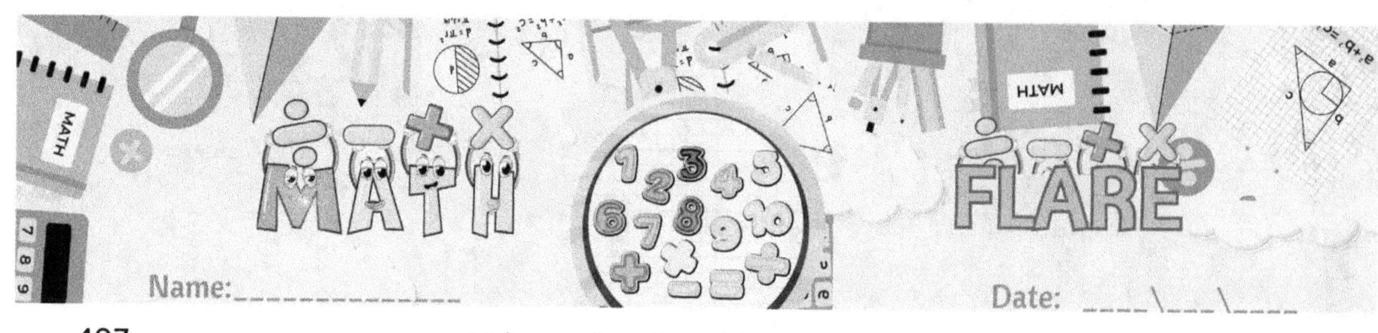

107. _________________ 5 hundreds + 7 tens + 8 ones + 5 tenths + 9 hundredths

108. _________________ 1 hundred + 4 tens + 5 ones + 5 hundredths

109. _________________ 2 hundreds + 7 tens + 7 ones + 6 tenths + 7 hundredths

110. _________________ 6 hundreds + 8 tens + 3 ones + 1 tenth + 3 hundredths

111. _________________ 2 hundreds + 9 tens + 8 ones + 8 tenths + 5 hundredths

112. _________________ 7 hundreds + 2 tens + 1 one + 7 tenths + 8 hundredths

113. _________________ 9 hundreds + 8 tens + 2 ones + 5 tenths + 2 hundredths

114. _________________ 3 hundreds + 3 tens + 6 ones + 4 tenths

115. _________________ 4 hundreds + 7 tens + 4 ones + 9 tenths + 2 hundredths

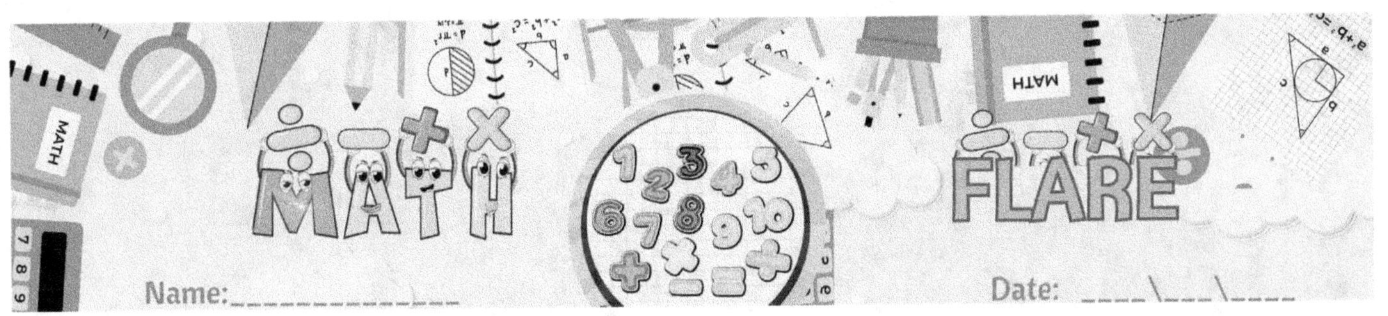

116. _________________ 5 hundreds + 9 tens + 3 tenths + 3 hundredths

117. _________________ 9 hundreds + 4 tens + 1 tenth

118. _________________ 7 hundreds + 7 tens + 6 ones + 9 tenths + 8 hundredths

119. _________________ 7 hundreds + 2 tens + 5 ones + 4 tenths + 2 hundredths

120. _________________ 9 hundreds + 7 tens + 8 ones + 4 tenths + 2 hundredths

121. _________________ 5 hundreds + 1 ten + 7 ones + 5 tenths + 9 hundredths

122. _________________ 5 hundreds + 9 tens + 6 ones + 5 hundredths

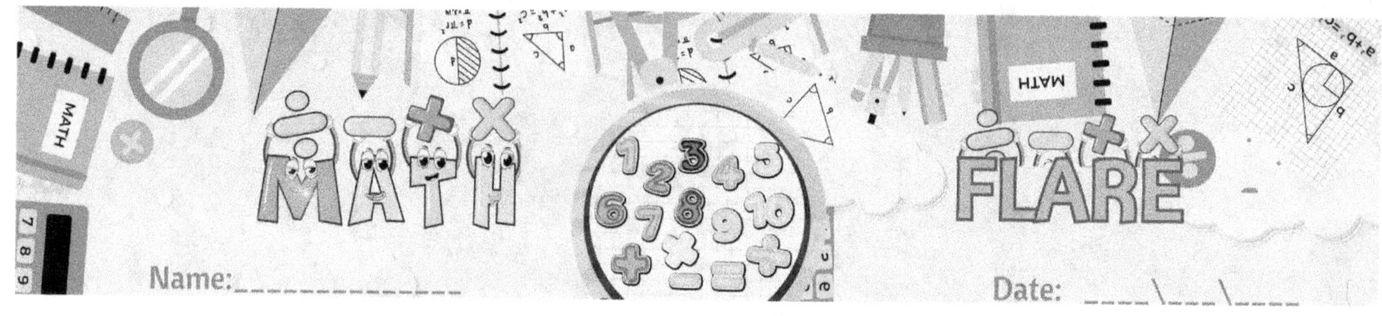

Place Value: Expanded Notation

Provide the expanded notation for each value.

123. 188.17 ______________________

124. 136.74 ______________________

125. 429.79 ______________________

126. 457.78 ______________________

127. 777.05 ______________________

128. 610.68 ______________________

129. 703.78 ______________________

130. 413.76 ______________________

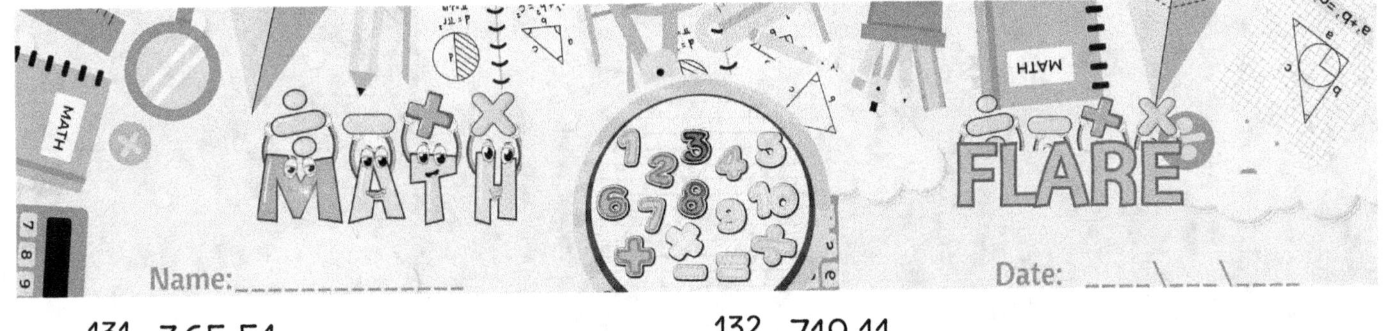

131. 365.51 _______________

132. 719.11 _______________

133. 172.56 _______________

134. 859.71 _______________

135. 938.69 _______________

136. 942.58 _______________

137. 127.99 _______________

138. 854.15 _______________

139. 860.91 ___________

140. 328.28 ___________

141. 983.63 ___________

142. 162.25 ___________

143. 251.39 ___________

144. 251.51 ___________

145. 576.26 ___________

146. 387.65 ___________

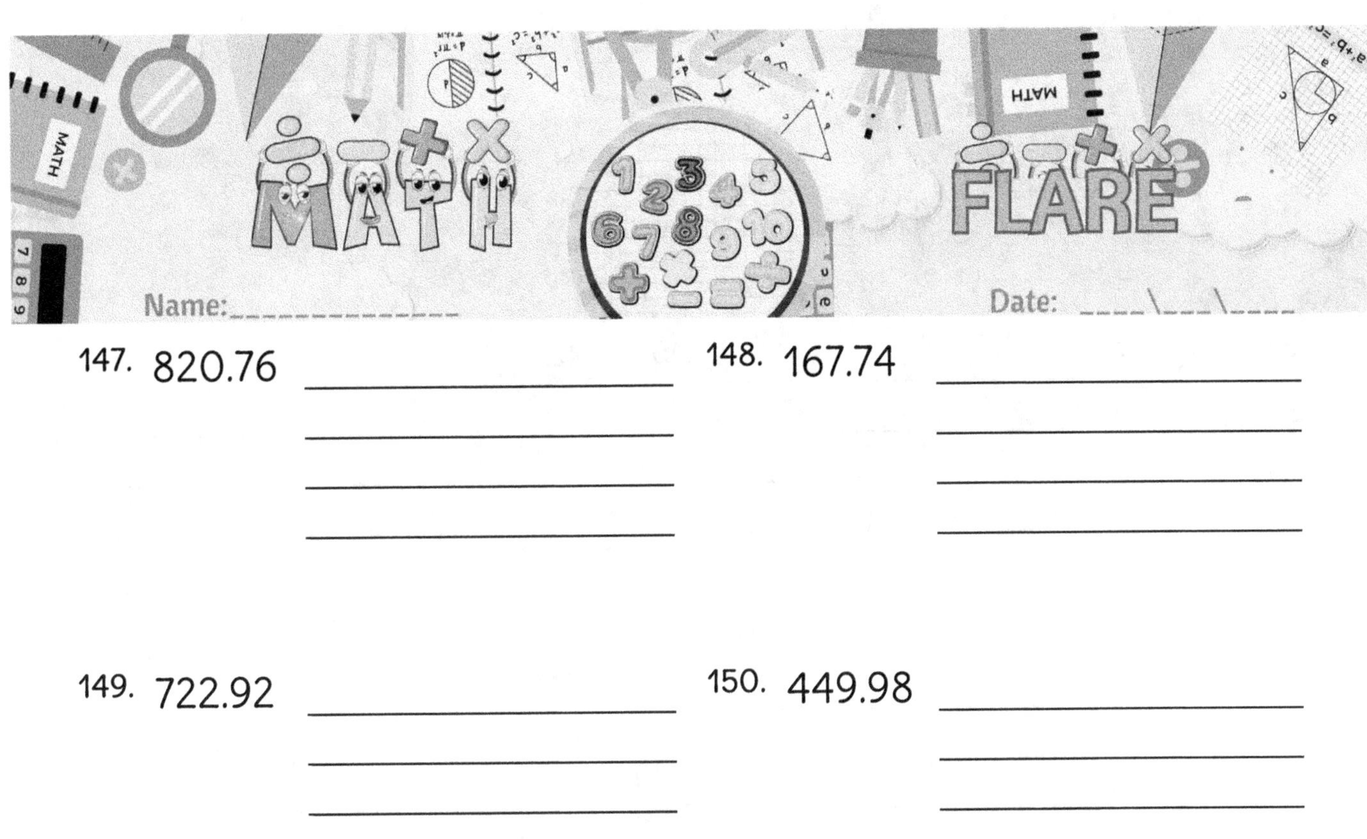

147. 820.76 ___________________

148. 167.74 ___________________

149. 722.92 ___________________

150. 449.98 ___________________

151. 930.66 ___________________

152. 204.31 ___________________

153. 542.44 ___________________

154. 570.53 ___________________

155. 868.33 __________________

156. 134.21 __________________

157. 921.47 __________________

158. 330.02 __________________

159. 913.43 __________________

160. 386.58 __________________

161. 934.78 __________________

162. 967.90 __________________

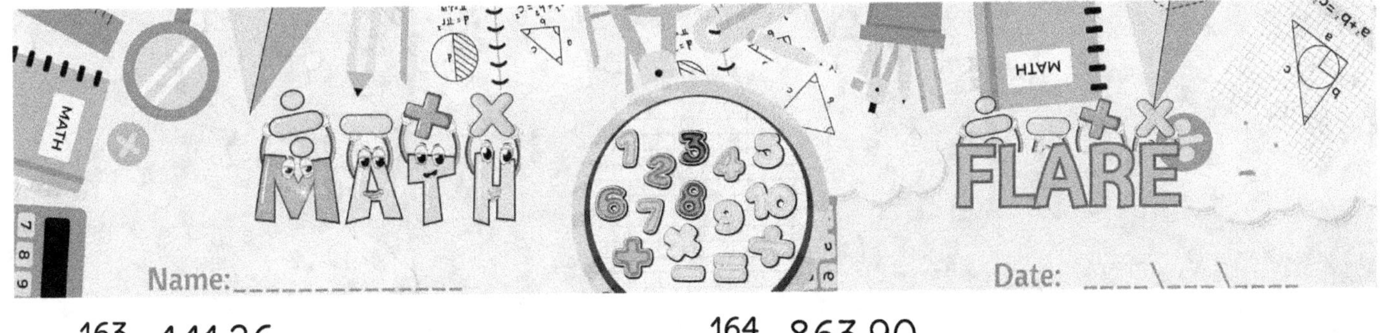

163. 441.26 _______________

164. 863.90 _______________

165. 417.62 _______________

166. 579.73 _______________

167. 649.21 _______________

168. 222.82 _______________

169. 397.70 _______________

170. 532.33 _______________

171. 562.34 _______________

172. 185.94 _______________

173. 916.07 _______________

174. 497.14 _______________

175. 994.78 _______________

176. 455.34 _______________

177. 444.66 _______________

178. 936.65 _______________

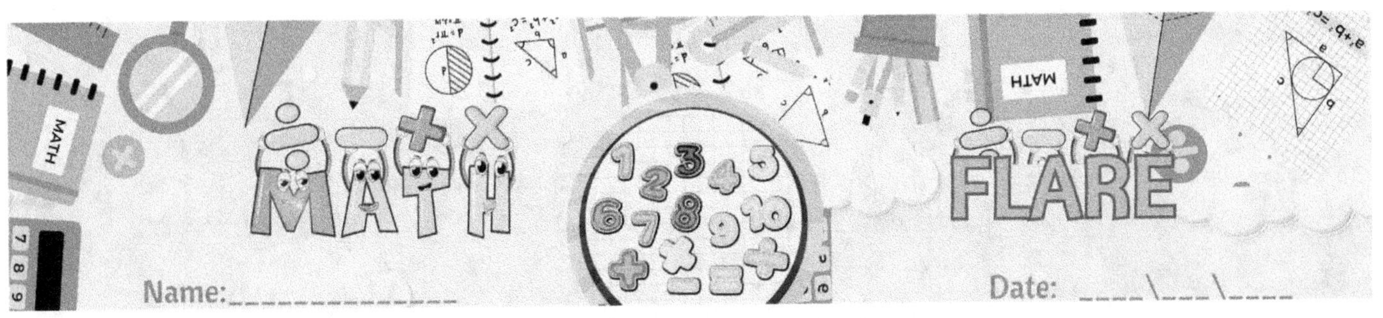

Place Value: Expanded Notation

Provide the expanded notation for each value.

179. __________________ 500 + 60 + 0.4 + 0.02

180. __________________ 100 + 40 + 2 + 0.1 + 0.04

181. __________________ 600 + 30 + 6 + 0.9 + 0.05

182. __________________ 700 + 9 + 0.2 + 0.04

183. __________________ 800 + 80 + 7 + 0.6 + 0.07

184. __________________ 300 + 50 + 3 + 0.7 + 0.07

185. __________________ 400 + 80 + 3 + 0.05

186. __________________ 200 + 60 + 1 + 0.1 + 0.09

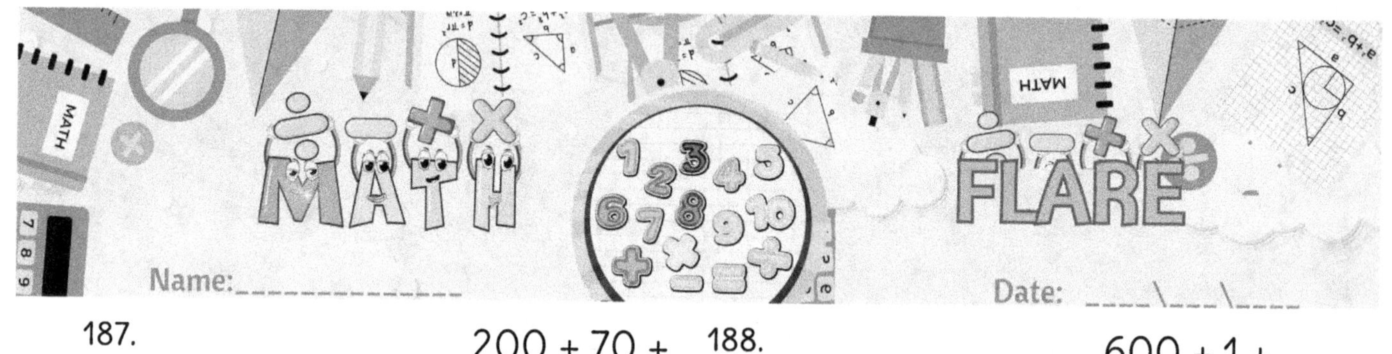

187. _________________ 200 + 70 + 6 + 0.6 + 0.05

188. _________________ 600 + 1 + 0.9 + 0.08

189. _________________ 900 + 90 + 1 + 0.2 + 0.07

190. _________________ 900 + 4 + 0.4

191. _________________ 100 + 20 + 1 + 0.1 + 0.01

192. _________________ 700 + 90 + 7 + 0.8 + 0.09

193. _________________ 900 + 40 + 0.6 + 0.03

194. _________________ 500 + 70 + 4 + 0.2 + 0.08

195. _________________ 300 + 90 + 3 + 0.4 + 0.06

196. _________________ 100 + 10 + 5 + 0.7 + 0.03

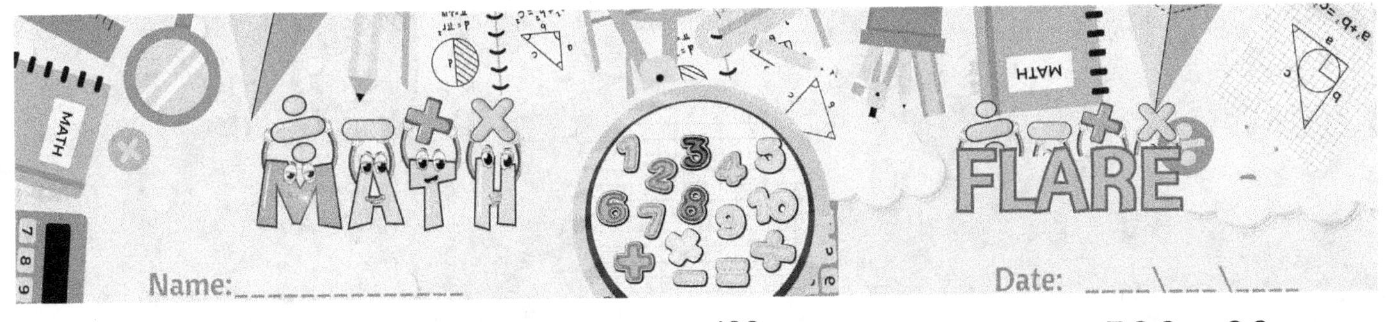

197. _______________ 700 + 20 + 0.9 + 0.02

198. _______________ 300 + 80 + 7 + 0.4 + 0.05

199. _______________ 800 + 30 + 3 + 0.8

200. _______________ 900 + 90 + 6 + 0.4 + 0.03

201. _______________ 700 + 30 + 8 + 0.3 + 0.07

202. _______________ 600 + 90 + 7 + 0.8 + 0.08

203. _______________ 700 + 60 + 9 + 0.9 + 0.07

204. _______________ 200 + 90 + 0.5 + 0.08

205. _______________ 800 + 80 + 7 + 0.5 + 0.05

206. _______________ 800 + 40 + 4 + 0.6 + 0.04

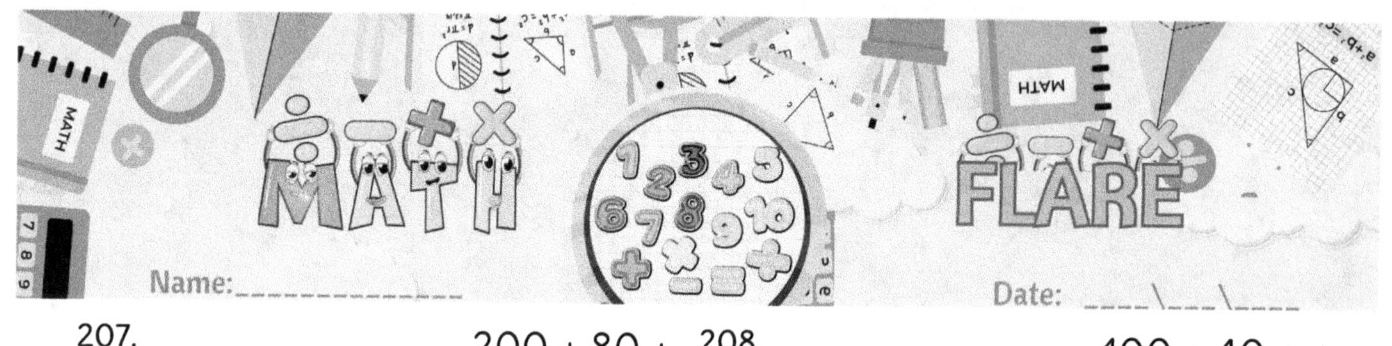

207. _____________ 200 + 80 + 8 + 0.2 + 0.01

208. _____________ 100 + 40 + 5 + 0.3

209. _____________ 500 + 70 + 5 + 0.6 + 0.09

210. _____________ 500 + 10 + 2 + 0.9 + 0.05

211. _____________ 600 + 80 + 9 + 0.4 + 0.08

212. _____________ 900 + 80 + 4 + 0.7 + 0.02

213. _____________ 700 + 60 + 9 + 0.4 + 0.08

214. _____________ 800 + 70 + 1 + 0.2 + 0.01

215. _____________ 700 + 40 + 9 + 0.4 + 0.09

216. _____________ 300 + 20 + 5 + 0.4 + 0.06

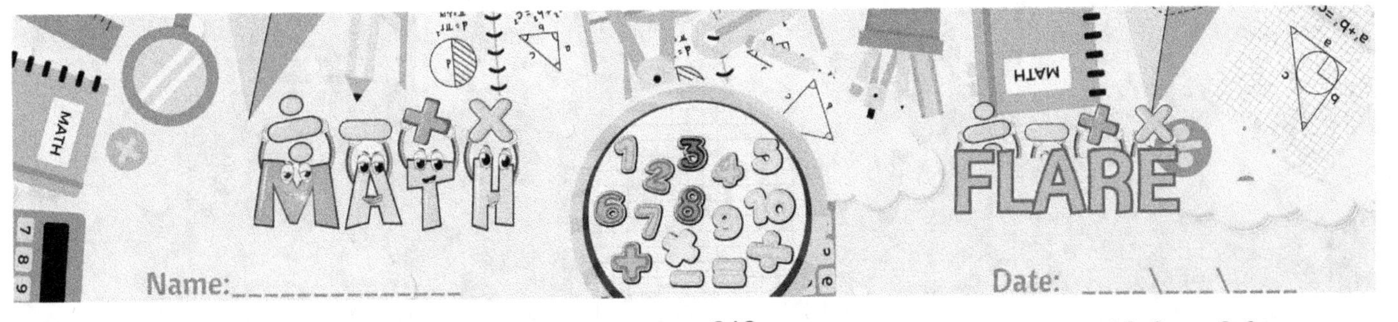

217. _____________ 100 + 80 + 0.1 + 0.05

218. _____________ 100 + 80 + 7 + 0.4 + 0.05

219. _____________ 400 + 80 + 0.7 + 0.08

220. _____________ 200 + 50 + 6 + 0.4

221. _____________ 400 + 3 + 0.04

222. _____________ 100 + 40 + 7 + 0.1 + 0.08

223. _____________ 200 + 30 + 1 + 0.4 + 0.03

224. _____________ 400 + 90 + 3 + 0.1 + 0.07

225. _____________ 500 + 10 + 1 + 0.1 + 0.08

226. _____________ 700 + 60 + 4 + 0.3 + 0.01

227. _______________ $200 + 40 + 5 + 0.2 + 0.01$

228. _______________ $400 + 40 + 1 + 0.7$

229. _______________ $200 + 3 + 0.6 + 0.04$

230. _______________ $900 + 70 + 8 + 0.9 + 0.07$

231. _______________ $700 + 30 + 4 + 0.2 + 0.08$

232. _______________ $100 + 50 + 7 + 0.1 + 0.08$

233. _______________ $200 + 2 + 0.7 + 0.07$

234. _______________ $500 + 60 + 3 + 0.9$

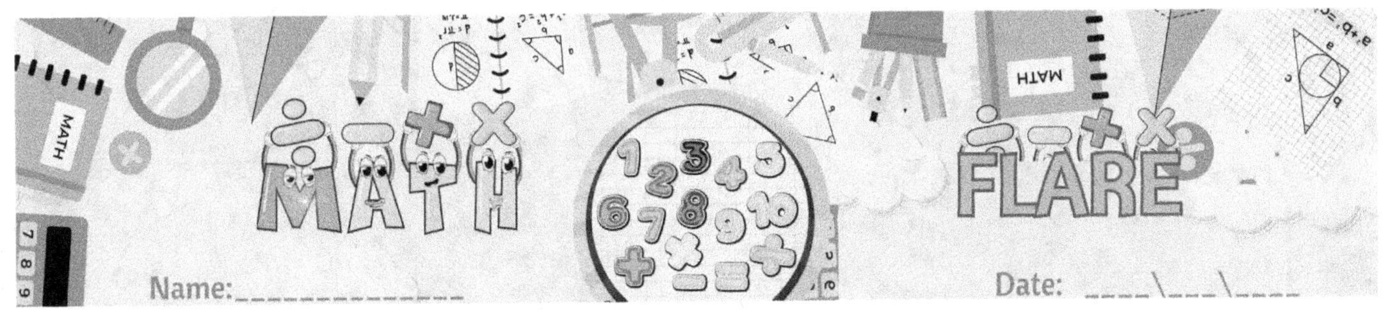

Place Value: Expanded Notation

Provide the expanded notation for each value.

235. 403.67 ________________

236. 938.97 ________________

237. 939.18 ________________

238. 697.09 ________________

239. 466.12 ________________

240. 638.30 ________________

241. 972.88 ________________

242. 231.35 ________________

243. 126.29 ________________

244. 578.32 ________________

245. 314.92 _________________
____

246. 136.29 _________________
____

247. 128.41 _________________
____

248. 169.41 _________________
____

249. 824.69 _________________
____

250. 168.00 _________________
____

251. 935.48 _________________
____

252. 633.47 _________________
____

253. 906.57 _________________
____

254. 677.39 _________________
____

255. 693.39 _________________
____

256. 691.18 _________________
____

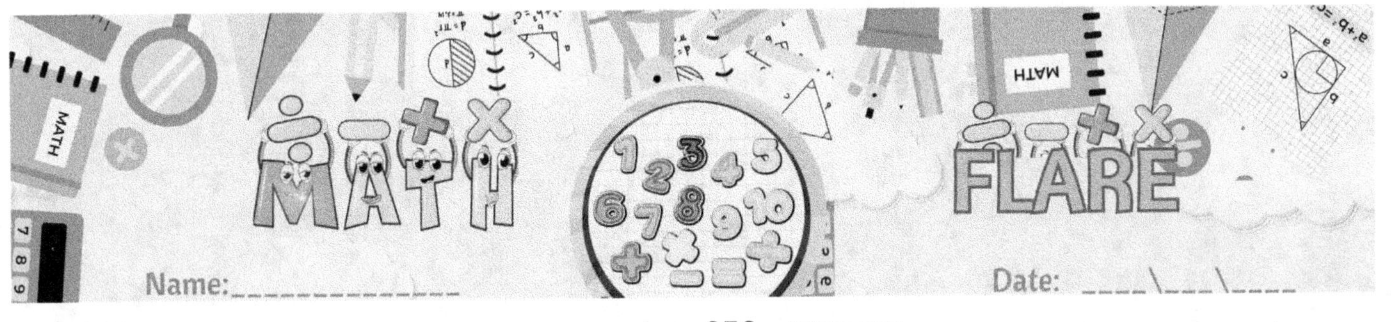

257. 566.45 _______________

258. 376.79 _______________

259. 779.29 _______________

260. 223.24 _______________

261. 699.43 _______________

262. 846.41 _______________

263. 941.56 _______________

264. 596.62 _______________

265. 778.58 _______________

266. 632.30 _______________

267. 881.95 _______________

268. 305.58 _______________

269. 567.54 ______________

270. 810.42 ______________

271. 386.18 ______________

272. 482.95 ______________

273. 721.23 ______________

274. 842.37 ______________

275. 283.43 ______________

276. 271.69 ______________

277. 120.89 ______________

278. 653.01 ______________

279. 278.25 ______________

280. 474.89 ______________

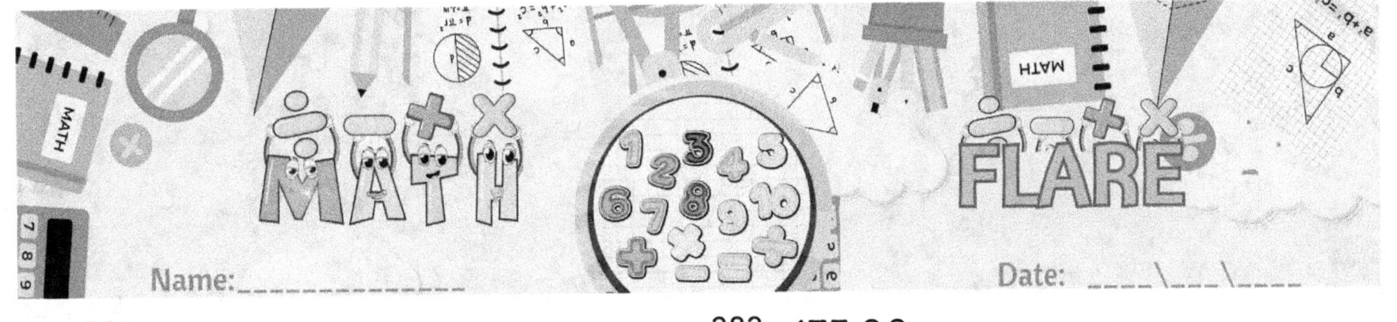

281. 735.90 _______________
____

282. 175.80 _______________
____

283. 616.92 _______________
____

284. 135.64 _______________
____

285. 143.49 _______________
____

286. 200.81 _______________
____

287. 250.51 _______________
____

288. 525.28 _______________
____

289. 870.41 _______________
____

290. 712.39 _______________
____

291. 472.52 _______________
____

292. 662.39 _______________
____

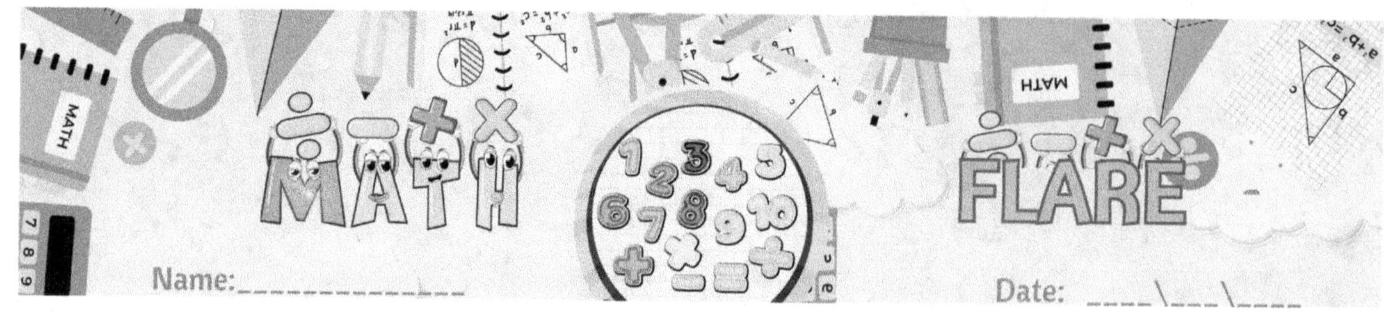

Place Value: Expanded Notation

Provide the expanded notation for each value.

293. _________________ nine hundred seventeen and seventy-eight hundredths

294. _________________ three hundred forty-two and ninety hundredths

295. _________________ nine hundred thirty-eight and eighty-five hundredths

296. _________________ two hundred twenty-six and forty-eight hundredths

297. _________________ two hundred eighty-nine and seventy hundredths

298. _______________ five hundred twenty-nine and sixty-one hundredths

299. _______________ seven hundred ninety-nine and seventy-one hundredths

300. _______________ six hundred eighty-two and fifty-eight hundredths

301. _______________ two hundred fifty-four and twenty-six hundredths

302. _______________ eight hundred twenty-two and eighty hundredths

303. _______________ six hundred one and eighty-two hundredths

304. _______________ one hundred fourteen and twenty-seven hundredths

305. _______________ seven hundred eighty-one and seventy-nine hundredths

306. _______________ five hundred fifty-two and fifty-seven hundredths

307. _______________ nine hundred twelve and twenty-two hundredths

308. _______________ one hundred sixty-four and twenty-one hundredths

309. _______________ four hundred ninety-four

310. _________________ five hundred twenty-one and seventy-four hundredths

311. _________________ six hundred seventy and thirty-five hundredths

312. _________________ nine hundred thirteen and forty-two hundredths

313. _________________ one hundred ninety-eight and fifty-five hundredths

314. _________________ four hundred four and forty-three hundredths

315. _________________ four hundred eighty-seven and twenty-eight hundredths

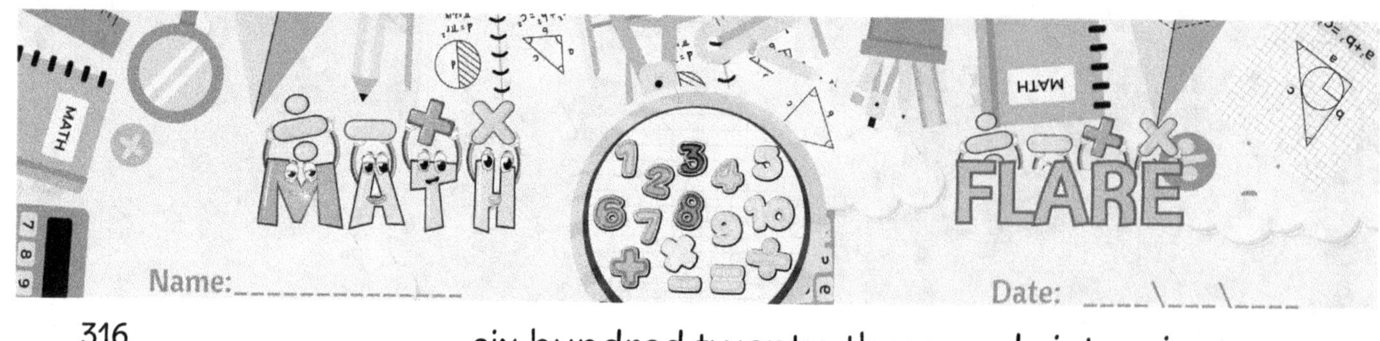

316. _______________ six hundred twenty-three and sixty-nine hundredths

317. _______________ three hundred twenty-nine and fifty-two hundredths

318. _______________ nine hundred six and one hundredth

319. _______________ five hundred fifty-three and seventeen hundredths

320. _______________ six hundred seventy-seven and eighty-three hundredths

321. _______________ four hundred eighty-one and eighty-three hundredths

322. _________________ four hundred fifty-six and seventy hundredths

323. _________________ four hundred thirty-five and eleven hundredths

324. _________________ eight hundred fifty-five and thirteen hundredths

325. _________________ four hundred thirty-seven and ninety-three hundredths

326. _________________ seven hundred twenty-three and seventy-six hundredths

327. _________________ five hundred sixty-five and twenty hundredths

328. _________________ four hundred seventy-eight and thirty-nine hundredths

329. _________________ nine hundred three and fifty-eight hundredths

330. _________________ one hundred fifty-six and ninety-seven hundredths

331. _________________ nine hundred eighty-two

332. _________________ five hundred ninety-one and twenty-seven hundredths

333. _________________ eight hundred fifty-three and thirty-four hundredths

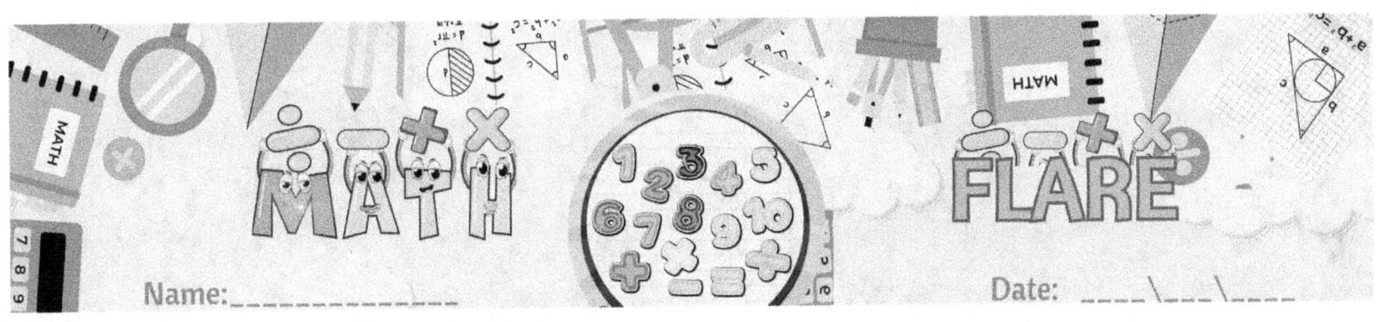

334. _________________ five hundred ninety-five and sixty-eight hundredths

335. _________________ three hundred twenty and sixty-seven hundredths

336. _________________ nine hundred thirteen and sixteen hundredths

337. _________________ five hundred seventy-three and ninety-seven hundredths

338. _________________ six hundred two and seventy hundredths

339. _________________ three hundred fifty-three and eighty-four hundredths

Name: _________________________   Date: ____________

340. _________________ five hundred ninety and ninety-two hundredths

341. _________________ two hundred eighty-eight and fifty-nine hundredths

342. _________________ one hundred eighty-six and thirty-two hundredths

343. _________________ one hundred thirty-one and thirty-two hundredths

344. _________________ four hundred forty-eight and seventy-five hundredths

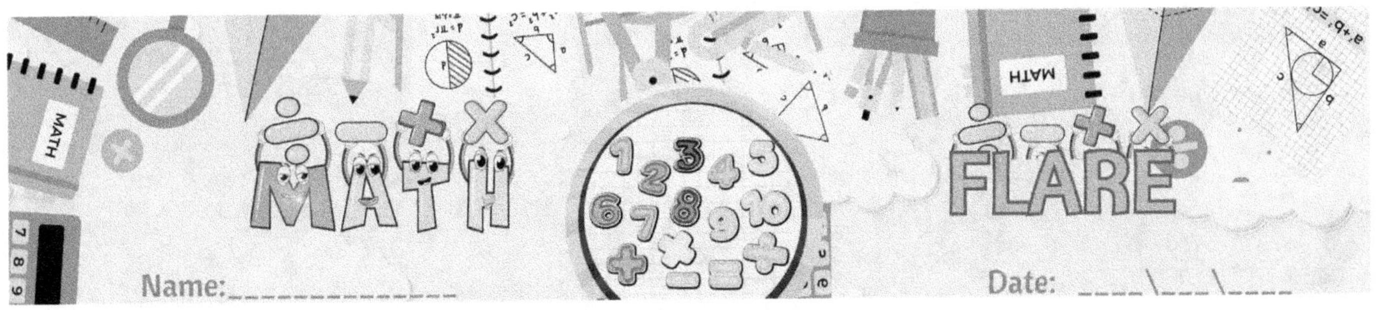

Place Value: Expanded Notation

Provide the expanded notation for each value.

345. 142.10 _________________

346. 559.13 _________________

347. 563.89 _________________

348. 613.35 _________________

349. 855.62 _________________

350. 415.17 _________________

351. 896.95 _________________

352. 383.69 _________________

353. 976.43 ________________

354. 221.89 ________________

355. 300.76 ________________

356. 797.54 ________________

357. 487.69 ________________

358. 746.69 ________________

359. 676.33 ________________

360. 158.03 ________________

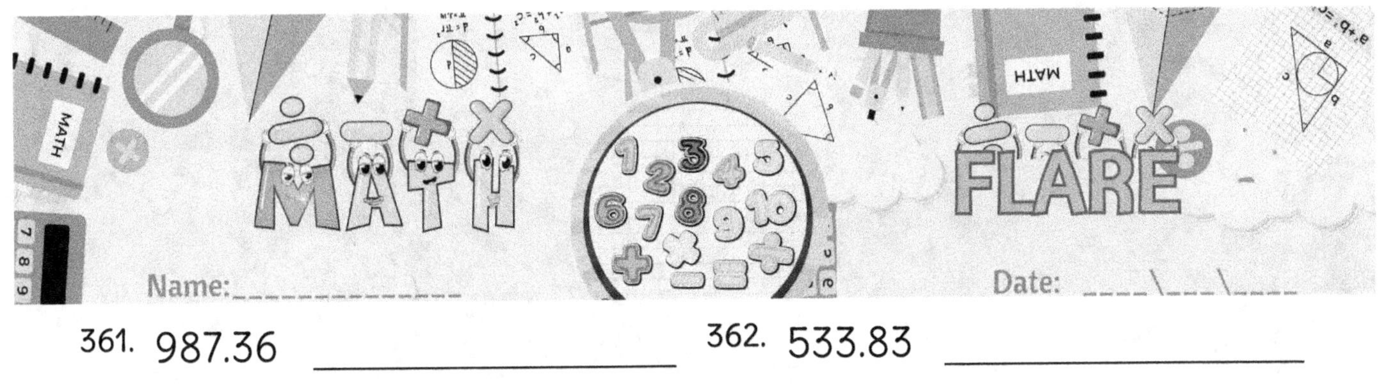

361. 987.36 _________________
____
____
____

362. 533.83 _________________
____
____
____

363. 260.62 _________________
____
____
____

364. 437.04 _________________
____
____
____

365. 539.73 _________________
____
____
____

366. 179.08 _________________
____
____
____

367. 160.07 _________________
____
____
____

368. 602.86 _________________
____
____
____

369. 183.76 ____________________

370. 574.11 ____________________

371. 149.72 ____________________

372. 726.81 ____________________

373. 652.16 ____________________

374. 962.25 ____________________

375. 489.24 ____________________

376. 395.51 ____________________

377. 425.39 ____________________

378. 986.35 ____________________

379. 813.03 ____________________

380. 878.79 ____________________

381. 259.87 ____________________

382. 951.84 ____________________

383. 622.76 ____________________

384. 588.41 ____________________

385. 260.00 ________________

386. 698.31 ________________

387. 614.83 ________________

388. 731.46 ________________

389. 394.92 ________________

390. 523.12 ________________

391. 525.46 ________________

392. 827.28 ________________

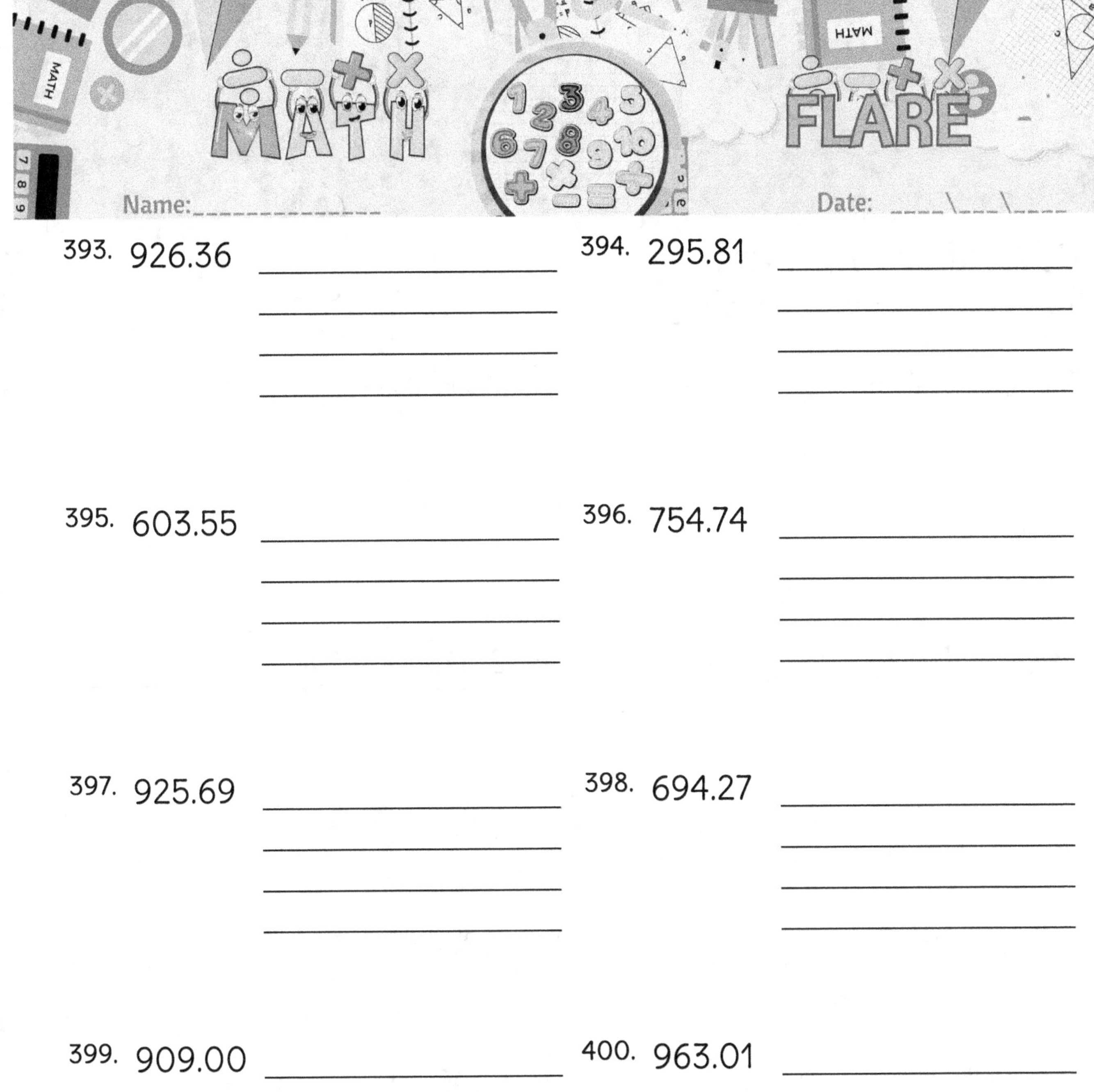

393. 926.36 _________________

394. 295.81 _________________

395. 603.55 _________________

396. 754.74 _________________

397. 925.69 _________________

398. 694.27 _________________

399. 909.00 _________________

400. 963.01 _________________

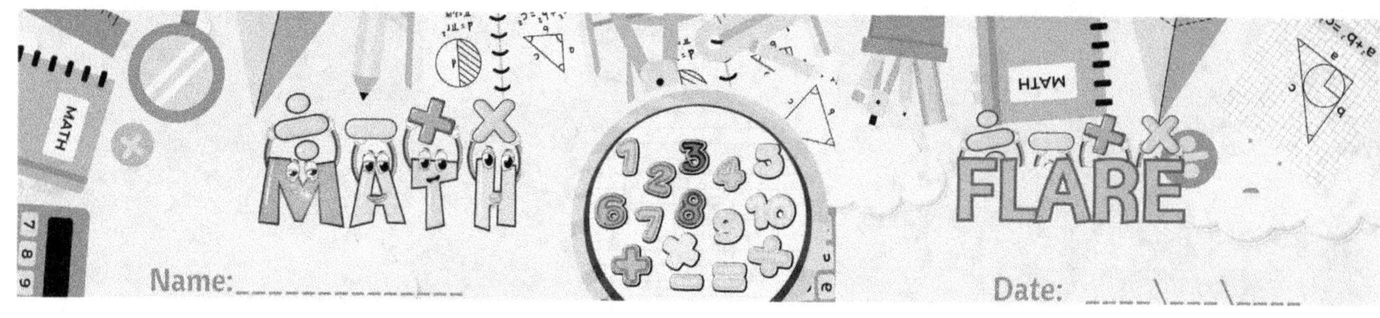

Rounding Numbers
Round to the underlined digit.

401. <u>4</u>,990.61 = _______________

402. <u>9</u>,610.31 = _______________

403. 5,2<u>9</u>5.97 = _______________

404. <u>3</u>,815.07 = _______________

405. 3,6<u>5</u>4.53 = _______________

406. <u>2</u>,701.50 = _______________

407. <u>7</u>,315.18 = _______________

408. <u>1</u>,141.87 = _______________

409. 7,<u>3</u>26.41 = _______________

410. 9,05<u>2</u>.46 = _______________

411. 4,72<u>1</u>.61 = _______________

412. 5,01<u>3</u>.39 = _______________

413. 9,33<u>6</u>.61 = _______________

414. 7,9<u>7</u>5.31 = _______________

415. 8,<u>9</u>81.65 = _______________

416. 1,<u>3</u>55.18 = _______________

417. 9,<u>1</u>10.68 = _______________

418. 6,7<u>2</u>1.98 = _______________

419. 2,7<u>7</u>0.38 = _______________

420. 8,4<u>1</u>4.22 = _______________

421. 5,<u>6</u>42.45 = _______________

422. <u>4</u>,286.08 = _______________

423. 3,0<u>7</u>9.38 = _______________

424. 6,60<u>6</u>.36 = _______________

425. <u>1</u>,486.52 = _______________

426. 3,<u>2</u>24.32 = _______________

427. 8,00<u>4</u>.40 = _______________

428. 4,56<u>3</u>.60 = _______________

429. 4,<u>5</u>87.02 = _______________

430. 7,<u>3</u>44.93 = _______________

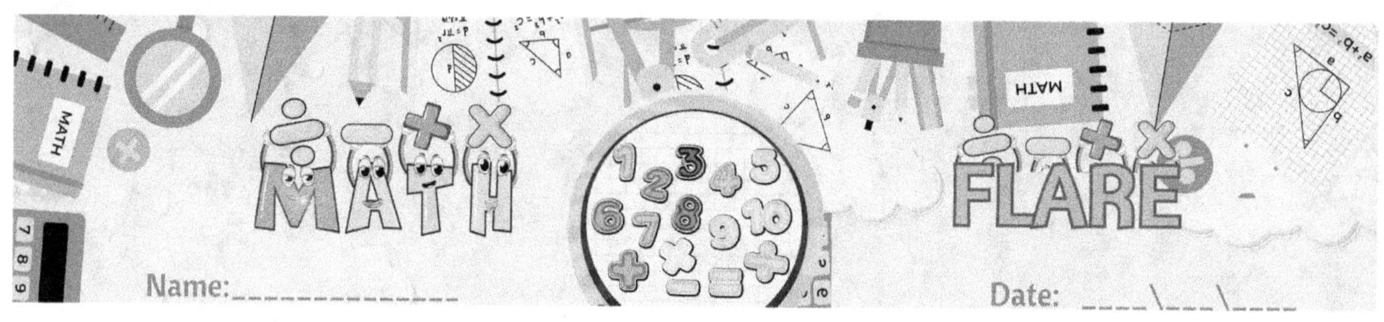

431. 4,<u>6</u>98.11 = _____________

432. 7,31<u>1</u>.16 = _____________

433. 1,<u>7</u>73.48 = _____________

434. 8,50<u>0</u>.11 = _____________

435. 4,797.<u>3</u>8 = _____________

436. <u>2</u>,988.34 = _____________

437. 5,22<u>2</u>.52 = _____________

438. <u>3</u>,412.60 = _____________

439. 3,2<u>2</u>9.67 = _____________

440. 9,89<u>8</u>.53 = _____________

441. <u>9</u>,667.96 = _____________

442. 6,006.<u>4</u>7 = _____________

443. 9,988.<u>2</u>3 = _____________

444. 4,89<u>6</u>.80 = _____________

445. 1,509.<u>6</u>1 = _____________

446. <u>1</u>,241.26 = _____________

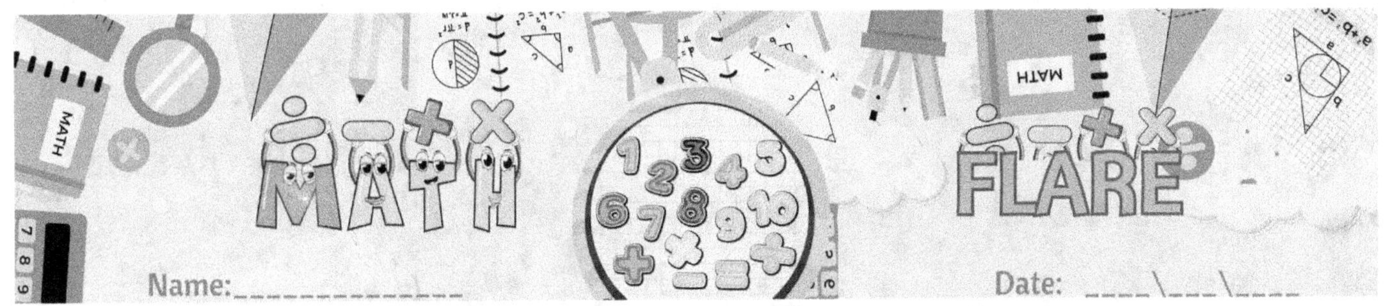

447. 8,9_36.21 = _______________

448. 2,2_88.41 = _______________

449. 3,97_6.45 = _______________

450. 5,68_0.35 = _______________

451. _8,436.82 = _______________

452. 3,_535.01 = _______________

453. _5,172.36 = _______________

454. 1,675._88 = _______________

455. 4,_987.75 = _______________

456. 1,704._53 = _______________

457. 7,53_0.94 = _______________

458. 8,689._60 = _______________

459. 3,328._56 = _______________

460. _1,430.20 = _______________

461. 4,_697.09 = _______________

462. 3,_751.58 = _______________

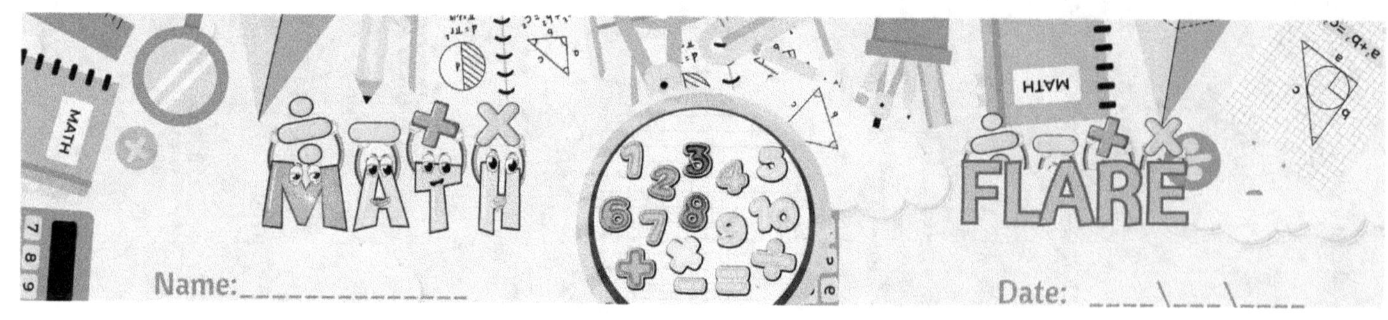

463. 6,554.<u>8</u>4 = _______________

464. 9,981.4<u>7</u> = _______________

465. 5,3<u>5</u>4.34 = _______________

466. <u>7</u>,410.44 = _______________

467. 4,<u>2</u>39.91 = _______________

468. <u>1</u>,836.50 = _______________

469. 4,17<u>7</u>.92 = _______________

470. 6,<u>9</u>93.31 = _______________

471. 6,1<u>3</u>2.65 = _______________

472. <u>6</u>,698.08 = _______________

473. 4,492.<u>3</u>1 = _______________

474. 2,871.<u>8</u>5 = _______________

475. 8,<u>7</u>46.25 = _______________

476. 9,6<u>3</u>5.97 = _______________

477. <u>4</u>,297.85 = _______________

478. 8,18<u>2</u>.56 = _______________

479. 6,09_6_.75 = ______________

480. _1_,245.25 = ______________

481. 4,288._1_0 = ______________

482. 6,7_1_5.99 = ______________

483. _1_,587.15 = ______________

484. 8,9_0_6.66 = ______________

485. _8_,908.11 = ______________

486. 2,163._1_0 = ______________

487. 3,1_3_8.80 = ______________

488. 1,0_9_7.60 = ______________

489. 4,5_1_2.36 = ______________

490. 4,092._8_5 = ______________

491. 5,4_5_7.39 = ______________

492. 6,53_2_.91 = ______________

493. 1,0_8_4.05 = ______________

494. 2,_7_99.46 = ______________

495. 6,2<u>0</u>1.44 = _______________

496. 6,91<u>6</u>.38 = _______________

497. 9,451.<u>6</u>2 = _______________

498. 1<u>,</u>006.76 = _______________

499. 9,<u>5</u>42.45 = _______________

500. 4,09<u>9</u>.15 = _______________

501. 7,001.<u>3</u>5 = _______________

502. 8,<u>0</u>99.72 = _______________

503. 8,11<u>0</u>.48 = _______________

504. 6,<u>9</u>83.13 = _______________

505. <u>9</u>,547.69 = _______________

506. 2,738.<u>7</u>4 = _______________

507. 9,0<u>4</u>2.70 = _______________

508. 3,<u>3</u>00.51 = _______________

509. 2,92<u>9</u>.61 = _______________

510. 5,35<u>1</u>.77 = _______________

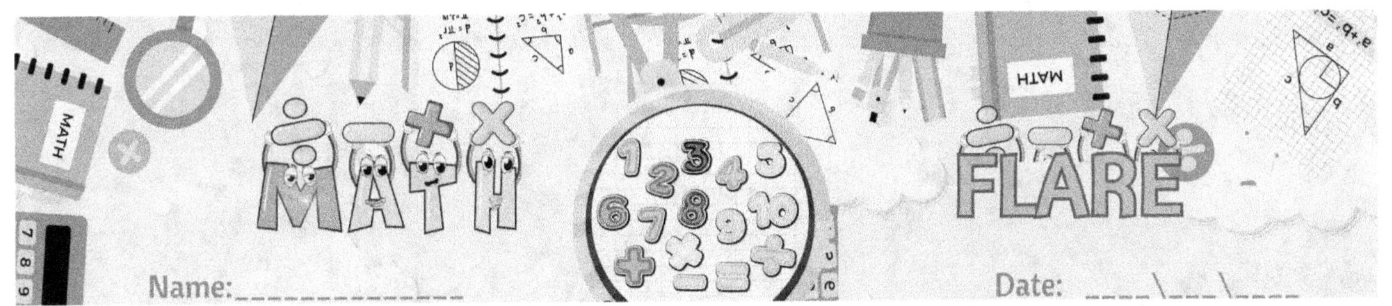

511. 7,40<u>6</u>.67 = _____________

512. 9,348.<u>3</u>7 = _____________

513. <u>3</u>,592.85 = _____________

514. 3,08<u>3</u>.30 = _____________

515. 7,<u>1</u>42.09 = _____________

516. 7,98<u>1</u>.09 = _____________

517. <u>3</u>,164.43 = _____________

518. 7,<u>6</u>48.17 = _____________

519. 2,07<u>3</u>.36 = _____________

520. 4,19<u>1</u>.24 = _____________

521. 5,2<u>7</u>1.64 = _____________

522. 4,142.<u>3</u>0 = _____________

523. 7,3<u>2</u>4.13 = _____________

524. 1,08<u>5</u>.07 = _____________

525. 2,535.<u>9</u>2 = _____________

526. 9,599.<u>7</u>2 = _____________

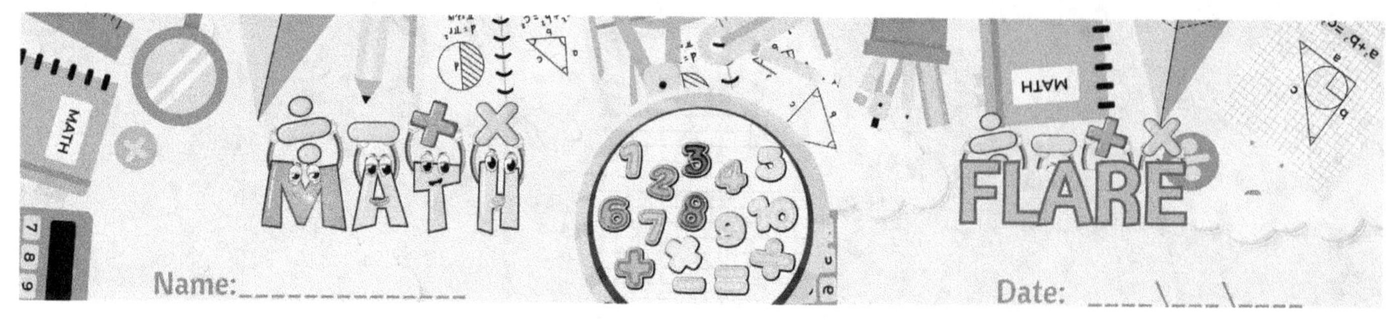

527. 6,614.0$\underline{0}$3 = _____________

528. 2,69$\underline{9}$2.84 = _____________

529. 6,$\underline{6}$70.40 = _____________

530. 2,8$\underline{2}$9.88 = _____________

531. 1,1$\underline{8}$4.35 = _____________

532. $\underline{4}$,291.08 = _____________

533. 8,64$\underline{0}$.10 = _____________

534. $\underline{2}$,997.59 = _____________

535. $\underline{4}$,243.90 = _____________

536. 6,18$\underline{8}$.38 = _____________

537. 8,605.5$\underline{0}$ = _____________

538. 4,60$\underline{4}$.01 = _____________

539. 9,3$\underline{5}$8.96 = _____________

540. 7,1$\underline{6}$9.37 = _____________

541. 3,1$\underline{2}$0.39 = _____________

542. 9,$\underline{8}$38.28 = _____________

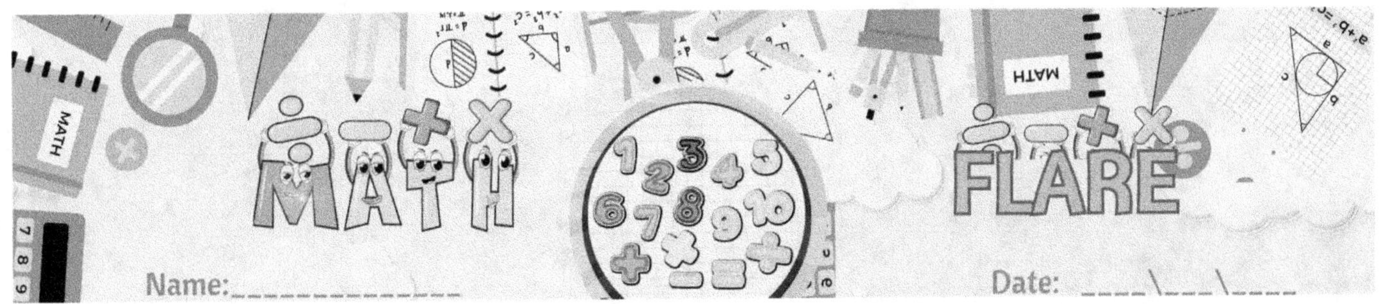

543. 8,167.98 = _________________

544. 9,160.58 = _________________

545. 6,686.17 = _________________

546. 6,109.02 = _________________

547. 3,940.06 = _________________

548. 8,000.73 = _________________

549. 5,657.36 = _________________

550. 8,220.34 = _________________

551. 4,751.94 = _________________

552. 2,803.45 = _________________

553. 8,933.39 = _________________

554. 6,351.21 = _________________

555. 8,827.50 = _________________

556. 3,859.04 = _________________

557. 1,775.59 = _________________

558. 8,025.41 = _________________

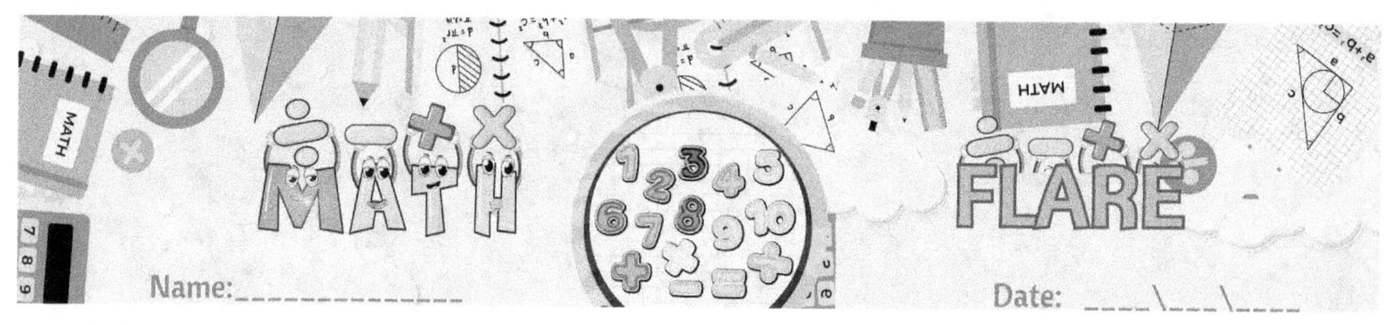

559. 5,4<u>4</u>7.21 = _______________

560. 9,<u>9</u>47.96 = _______________

561. <u>6</u>,124.70 = _______________

562. 7,349.<u>8</u>5 = _______________

563. <u>6</u>,630.10 = _______________

564. <u>1</u>,099.74 = _______________

565. <u>5</u>,167.42 = _______________

566. 4,11<u>5</u>.59 = _______________

567. 1,7<u>0</u>8.26 = _______________

568. <u>1</u>,595.26 = _______________

569. 8,8<u>3</u>9.40 = _______________

570. 1,9<u>5</u>3.72 = _______________

571. 9,375.<u>5</u>7 = _______________

572. 8,5<u>6</u>0.41 = _______________

573. 8,28<u>9</u>.21 = _______________

574. 4,9<u>0</u>3.99 = _______________

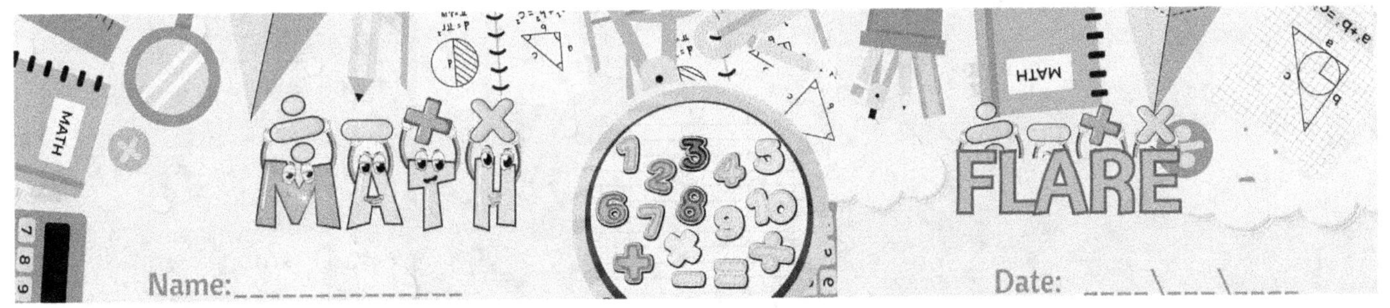

575. 2,070.85 = _____________

576. 5,433.35 = _____________

577. 5,974.31 = _____________

578. 8,163.54 = _____________

579. 4,398.89 = _____________

580. 6,426.89 = _____________

581. 6,659.66 = _____________

582. 8,613.29 = _____________

583. 7,035.47 = _____________

584. 8,450.04 = _____________

585. 8,077.93 = _____________

586. 8,380.89 = _____________

587. 5,357.68 = _____________

588. 3,288.89 = _____________

589. 4,170.08 = _____________

590. 1,384.85 = _____________

ANSWERS

Page 1: Place Value

1. 6 tens

2. 5 tens

3. 7 ones

4. 9 tens

5. 4 hundredths

6. 9 hundredths

7. 9 ones

8. 5 hundreds

9. 2 hundreds

10. 2 tenths

11. 9 tens

12. 6 tenths

13. 0 tens

14. 1 ten

15. 1 tenth

16. 1 tenth

17. 7 tens

18. 0 tens

19. 8 ones

20. 3 tenths

21. 5 hundreds

22. 2 tens

23. 6 hundreds

24. 3 ones

25. 8 hundreds

26. 1 one

27. 7 tenths

28. 3 hundreds

29. 2 hundreds

30. 9 hundredths

31. 2 ones

32. 0 tenths

33. 9 ones

34. 7 tenths

35. 9 tenths

36. 4 tenths

37. 4 tenths

38. 5 tenths

39. 6 tens

40. 8 hundredths

41. 7 hundreds

42. 8 ones

43. 1 tenth

44. 8 hundredths

45. 2 hundreds

46. 3 tenths

47. 6 hundredths

48. 7 hundredths

49. 8 hundredths

50. 8 hundreds

51. 1 hundredth

52. 9 tenths

53. 6 tens

54. 7 ones

55. 1 tenth

56. 9 hundreds

57. 3 tens

58. 1 hundred   59. 6 tenths   60. 6 ones

61. 7 hundredths   62. 2 hundreds

Page 5: Place Value: Expanded Notation

63. 382.27   64. 665.55   65. 540.67   66. 624.90   67. 925.11

68. 922.81   69. 811.85   70. 439.23   71. 261.09   72. 181.21

73. 708.53   74. 644.11   75. 284.54   76. 246.81   77. 886.98

78. 621.53   79. 245.65   80. 568.96   81. 952.23   82. 394.75

83. 197.40   84. 605.27   85. 940.12   86. 562.23   87. 207.31

88. 429.06   89. 834.64   90. 775.11   91. 109.44   92. 803.30

93. 404.15   94. 197.85   95. 940.32   96. 870.77   97. 881.29

98. 267.87   99. 548.96   100. 385.93   101. 630.26   102. 109.65

103. 366.76   104. 343.24   105. 744.36   106. 711.84   107. 578.59

108. 145.05   109. 277.67   110. 683.13   111. 298.85   112. 721.78

113. 982.52   114. 336.40   115. 474.92   116. 590.33   117. 940.10

118. 776.98   119. 725.42   120. 978.42   121. 517.59   122. 596.05

Page 12: Place Value: Expanded Notation

123. 1 hundred + 8 tens + 8 ones + 1 tenth + 7 hundredths

124. 1 hundred + 3 tens + 6 ones + 7 tenths + 4 hundredths

125. 4 hundreds + 2 tens + 9 ones + 7 tenths + 9 hundredths

126. 4 hundreds + 5 tens + 7 ones + 7 tenths + 8 hundredths

127. 7 hundreds + 7 tens + 7 ones + 5 hundredths

128. 6 hundreds + 1 ten + 6 tenths + 8 hundredths

129. 7 hundreds + 3 ones + 7 tenths + 8 hundredths

130. 4 hundreds + 1 ten + 3 ones + 7 tenths + 6 hundredths

131. 3 hundreds + 6 tens + 5 ones + 5 tenths + 1 hundredth

132. 7 hundreds + 1 ten + 9 ones + 1 tenth + 1 hundredth

133. 1 hundred + 7 tens + 2 ones + 5 tenths + 6 hundredths

134. 8 hundreds + 5 tens + 9 ones + 7 tenths + 1 hundredth

135. 9 hundreds + 3 tens + 8 ones + 6 tenths + 9 hundredths

136. 9 hundreds + 4 tens + 2 ones + 5 tenths + 8 hundredths

137. 1 hundred + 2 tens + 7 ones + 9 tenths + 9 hundredths

138. 8 hundreds + 5 tens + 4 ones + 1 tenth + 5 hundredths

139. 8 hundreds + 6 tens + 9 tenths + 1 hundredth

140. 3 hundreds + 2 tens + 8 ones + 2 tenths + 8 hundredths

141. 9 hundreds + 8 tens + 3 ones + 6 tenths + 3 hundredths

142. 1 hundred + 6 tens + 2 ones + 2 tenths + 5 hundredths

143. 2 hundreds + 5 tens + 1 one + 3 tenths + 9 hundredths

144. 2 hundreds + 5 tens + 1 one + 5 tenths + 1 hundredth

145. 5 hundreds + 7 tens + 6 ones + 2 tenths + 6 hundredths

146. 3 hundreds + 8 tens + 7 ones + 6 tenths + 5 hundredths

147. 8 hundreds + 2 tens + 7 tenths + 6 hundredths

148. 1 hundred + 6 tens + 7 ones + 7 tenths + 4 hundredths

149. 7 hundreds + 2 tens + 2 ones + 9 tenths + 2 hundredths

150. 4 hundreds + 4 tens + 9 ones + 9 tenths + 8 hundredths

151. 9 hundreds + 3 tens + 6 tenths + 6 hundredths

152. 2 hundreds + 4 ones + 3 tenths + 1 hundredth

153. 5 hundreds + 4 tens + 2 ones + 4 tenths + 4 hundredths

154. 5 hundreds + 7 tens + 5 tenths + 3 hundredths

155. 8 hundreds + 6 tens + 8 ones + 3 tenths + 3 hundredths

156. 1 hundred + 3 tens + 4 ones + 2 tenths + 1 hundredth

157. 9 hundreds + 2 tens + 1 one + 4 tenths + 7 hundredths

158. 3 hundreds + 3 tens + 2 hundredths

159. 9 hundreds + 1 ten + 3 ones + 4 tenths + 3 hundredths

160. 3 hundreds + 8 tens + 6 ones + 5 tenths + 8 hundredths

161. 9 hundreds + 3 tens + 4 ones + 7 tenths + 8 hundredths

162. 9 hundreds + 6 tens + 7 ones + 9 tenths

163. 4 hundreds + 4 tens + 1 one + 2 tenths + 6 hundredths

164. 8 hundreds + 6 tens + 3 ones + 9 tenths

165. 4 hundreds + 1 ten + 7 ones + 6 tenths + 2 hundredths

166. 5 hundreds + 7 tens + 9 ones + 7 tenths + 3 hundredths

167. 6 hundreds + 4 tens + 9 ones + 2 tenths + 1 hundredth

168. 2 hundreds + 2 tens + 2 ones + 8 tenths + 2 hundredths

169. 3 hundreds + 9 tens + 7 ones + 7 tenths

170. 5 hundreds + 3 tens + 2 ones + 3 tenths + 3 hundredths

171. 5 hundreds + 6 tens + 2 ones + 3 tenths + 4 hundredths

172. 1 hundred + 8 tens + 5 ones + 9 tenths + 4 hundredths

173. 9 hundreds + 1 ten + 6 ones + 7 hundredths

174. 4 hundreds + 9 tens + 7 ones + 1 tenth + 4 hundredths

175. 9 hundreds + 9 tens + 4 ones + 7 tenths + 8 hundredths

176. 4 hundreds + 5 tens + 5 ones + 3 tenths + 4 hundredths

177. 4 hundreds + 4 tens + 4 ones + 6 tenths + 6 hundredths

178. 9 hundreds + 3 tens + 6 ones + 6 tenths + 5 hundredths

Page 19: Place Value: Expanded Notation

179. 560.42	180. 142.14	181. 636.95	182. 709.24	183. 887.67
184. 353.77	185. 483.05	186. 261.19	187. 276.65	188. 601.98
189. 991.27	190. 904.40	191. 121.11	192. 797.89	193. 940.63
194. 574.28	195. 393.46	196. 115.73	197. 720.92	198. 387.45
199. 833.80	200. 996.43	201. 738.37	202. 697.88	203. 769.97
204. 290.58	205. 887.55	206. 844.64	207. 288.21	208. 145.30
209. 575.69	210. 512.95	211. 689.48	212. 984.72	213. 769.48
214. 871.21	215. 749.49	216. 325.46	217. 180.15	218. 187.45
219. 480.78	220. 256.40	221. 403.04	222. 147.18	223. 231.43
224. 493.17	225. 511.18	226. 764.31	227. 245.21	228. 441.70
229. 203.64	230. 978.97	231. 734.28	232. 157.18	233. 202.77

234. 563.90

Page 25: Place Value: Expanded Notation

235. 400 + 3 + 0.6 + 0.07

236. 900 + 30 + 8 + 0.9 + 0.07

237. 900 + 30 + 9 + 0.1 + 0.08

238. 600 + 90 + 7 + 0.09

239. 400 + 60 + 6 + 0.1 + 0.02

240. 600 + 30 + 8 + 0.3

241. 900 + 70 + 2 + 0.8 + 0.08

242. 200 + 30 + 1 + 0.3 + 0.05

243. 100 + 20 + 6 + 0.2 + 0.09

244. 500 + 70 + 8 + 0.3 + 0.02

245. 300 + 10 + 4 + 0.9 + 0.02

246. 100 + 30 + 6 + 0.2 + 0.09

247. 100 + 20 + 8 + 0.4 + 0.01

248. 100 + 60 + 9 + 0.4 + 0.01

249. 800 + 20 + 4 + 0.6 + 0.09

250. 100 + 60 + 8

251. 900 + 30 + 5 + 0.4 + 0.08

252. 600 + 30 + 3 + 0.4 + 0.07

253. 900 + 6 + 0.5 + 0.07

254. 600 + 70 + 7 + 0.3 + 0.09

255. 600 + 90 + 3 + 0.3 + 0.09

256. 600 + 90 + 1 + 0.1 + 0.08

257. 500 + 60 + 6 + 0.4 + 0.05

258. 300 + 70 + 6 + 0.7 + 0.09

259. 700 + 70 + 9 + 0.2 + 0.09

260. 200 + 20 + 3 + 0.2 + 0.04

261. 600 + 90 + 9 + 0.4 + 0.03

262. 800 + 40 + 6 + 0.4 + 0.01

263. 900 + 40 + 1 + 0.5 + 0.06

264. 500 + 90 + 6 + 0.6 + 0.02

265. 700 + 70 + 8 + 0.5 + 0.08

266. 600 + 30 + 2 + 0.3

267. 800 + 80 + 1 + 0.9 + 0.05

268. 300 + 5 + 0.5 + 0.08

269. 500 + 60 + 7 + 0.5 + 0.04

270. 800 + 10 + 0.4 + 0.02

271. 300 + 80 + 6 + 0.1 + 0.08

272. 400 + 80 + 2 + 0.9 + 0.05

273. 700 + 20 + 1 + 0.2 + 0.03

274. 800 + 40 + 2 + 0.3 + 0.07

275. 200 + 80 + 3 + 0.4 + 0.03

276. 200 + 70 + 1 + 0.6 + 0.09

277. 100 + 20 + 0.8 + 0.09

278. 600 + 50 + 3 + 0.01

279. 200 + 70 + 8 + 0.2 + 0.05

280. 400 + 70 + 4 + 0.8 + 0.09

281. 700 + 30 + 5 + 0.9

282. 100 + 70 + 5 + 0.8

283. 600 + 10 + 6 + 0.9 + 0.02

284. 100 + 30 + 5 + 0.6 + 0.04

285. 100 + 40 + 3 + 0.4 + 0.09

286. 200 + 0.8 + 0.01

287. 200 + 50 + 0.5 + 0.01

288. 500 + 20 + 5 + 0.2 + 0.08

289. 800 + 70 + 0.4 + 0.01

290. 700 + 10 + 2 + 0.3 + 0.09

291. 400 + 70 + 2 + 0.5 + 0.02

292. 600 + 60 + 2 + 0.3 + 0.09

Page 30: Place Value: Expanded Notation

293. 917.78
294. 342.90
295. 938.85
296. 226.48
297. 289.70

298. 529.61
299. 799.71
300. 682.58
301. 254.26
302. 822.80

303. 601.82
304. 114.27
305. 781.79
306. 552.57
307. 912.22

308. 164.21
309. 494.00
310. 521.74
311. 670.35
312. 913.42

313. 198.55
314. 404.43
315. 487.28
316. 623.69
317. 329.52

318. 906.01
319. 553.17
320. 677.83
321. 481.83
322. 456.70

323. 435.11
324. 855.13
325. 437.93
326. 723.76
327. 565.20

328. 478.39
329. 903.58
330. 156.97
331. 982.00
332. 591.27

333. 853.34
334. 595.68
335. 320.67
336. 913.16
337. 573.97

338. 602.70
339. 353.84
340. 590.92
341. 288.59
342. 186.32

343. 131.32   344. 448.75

Page 39: Place Value: Expanded Notation

345. one hundred forty-two and ten hundredths

346. five hundred fifty-nine and thirteen hundredths

347. five hundred sixty-three and eighty-nine hundredths

348. six hundred thirteen and thirty-five hundredths

349. eight hundred fifty-five and sixty-two hundredths

350. four hundred fifteen and seventeen hundredths

351. eight hundred ninety-six and ninety-five hundredths

352. three hundred eighty-three and sixty-nine hundredths

353. nine hundred seventy-six and forty-three hundredths

354. two hundred twenty-one and eighty-nine hundredths

355. three hundred and seventy-six hundredths

356. seven hundred ninety-seven and fifty-four hundredths

357. four hundred eighty-seven and sixty-nine hundredths

358. seven hundred forty-six and sixty-nine hundredths

359. six hundred seventy-six and thirty-three hundredths

360. one hundred fifty-eight and three hundredths

361. nine hundred eighty-seven and thirty-six hundredths

362. five hundred thirty-three and eighty-three hundredths

363. two hundred sixty and sixty-two hundredths

364. four hundred thirty-seven and four hundredths

365. five hundred thirty-nine and seventy-three hundredths

366. one hundred seventy-nine and eight hundredths

367. one hundred sixty and seven hundredths

368. six hundred two and eighty-six hundredths

369. one hundred eighty-three and seventy-six hundredths

370. five hundred seventy-four and eleven hundredths

371. one hundred forty-nine and seventy-two hundredths

372. seven hundred twenty-six and eighty-one hundredths

373. six hundred fifty-two and sixteen hundredths

374. nine hundred sixty-two and twenty-five hundredths

375. four hundred eighty-nine and twenty-four hundredths

376. three hundred ninety-five and fifty-one hundredths

377. four hundred twenty-five and thirty-nine hundredths

378. nine hundred eighty-six and thirty-five hundredths

379. eight hundred thirteen and three hundredths

380. eight hundred seventy-eight and seventy-nine hundredths

381. two hundred fifty-nine and eighty-seven hundredths

382. nine hundred fifty-one and eighty-four hundredths

383. six hundred twenty-two and seventy-six hundredths

384. five hundred eighty-eight and forty-one hundredths

385. two hundred sixty

386. six hundred ninety-eight and thirty-one hundredths

387. six hundred fourteen and eighty-three hundredths

388. seven hundred thirty-one and forty-six hundredths

389. three hundred ninety-four and ninety-two hundredths

390. five hundred twenty-three and twelve hundredths

391. five hundred twenty-five and forty-six hundredths

392. eight hundred twenty-seven and twenty-eight hundredths

393. nine hundred twenty-six and thirty-six hundredths

394. two hundred ninety-five and eighty-one hundredths

395. six hundred three and fifty-five hundredths

396. seven hundred fifty-four and seventy-four hundredths

397. nine hundred twenty-five and sixty-nine hundredths

398. six hundred ninety-four and twenty-seven hundredths

399. nine hundred nine

400. nine hundred sixty-three and one hundredth

Page 46: Rounding Numbers

401. 5,000	402. 10,000	403. 5,300	404. 4,000	405. 3,650
406. 3,000	407. 7,000	408. 1,000	409. 7,300	410. 9,052
411. 4,722	412. 5,013	413. 9,337	414. 7,980	415. 9,000
416. 1,400	417. 9,100	418. 6,720	419. 2,770	420. 8,410

421. 5,600   422. 4,000   423. 3,080   424. 6,606   425. 1,000

426. 3,200   427. 8,004   428. 4,564   429. 4,600   430. 7,300

431. 4,700   432. 7,311   433. 1,800   434. 8,500   435. 4,797.4

436. 3,000   437. 5,223   438. 3,000   439. 3,230   440. 9,899

441. 10,000   442. 6,006.5 443. 9,988.2 444. 4,897   445. 1,509.6

446. 1,000   447. 8,900   448. 2,300   449. 3,976   450. 5,680

451. 8,000   452. 3,500   453. 5,000   454. 1,675.9 455. 5,000

456. 1,704.5 457. 7,531   458. 8,689.6 459. 3,328.6 460. 1,000

461. 4,700   462. 3,800   463. 6,554.8 464. 9,981.5 465. 5,350

466. 7,000   467. 4,200   468. 2,000   469. 4,178   470. 7,000

471. 6,130   472. 7,000   473. 4,492.3 474. 2,872   475. 8,700

476. 9,640   477. 4,000   478. 8,183   479. 6,097   480. 1,000

481. 4,288.1 482. 6,720   483. 2,000   484. 8,910   485. 9,000

486. 2,163.1 487. 3,140   488. 1,100   489. 4,510   490. 4,092.9

491. 5,460   492. 6,533   493. 1,100   494. 2,800   495. 6,200

496. 6,916   497. 9,451.6 498. 1,000   499. 9,500   500. 4,099

501. 7,001.4 502. 8,100   503. 8,110   504. 7,000   505. 10,000

506. 2,738.7 507. 9,040   508. 3,300   509. 2,930   510. 5,352

511. 7,407   512. 9,348.4 513. 4,000   514. 3,083   515. 7,100

516. 7,981   517. 3,000   518. 7,600   519. 2,073   520. 4,191

521. 5,270   522. 4,142.3 523. 7,320   524. 1,085   525. 2,535.9

526. 9,599.7   527. 6,614   528. 2,690   529. 6,700   530. 2,830

531. 1,180   532. 4,000   533. 8,640   534. 3,000   535. 4,000

536. 6,188   537. 8,605.5   538. 4,604   539. 9,360   540. 7,200

541. 3,120   542. 9,800   543. 8,168   544. 9,160.6   545. 7,000

546. 6,110   547. 3,940   548. 8,000   549. 6,000   550. 8,220

551. 4,750   552. 2,803   553. 8,900   554. 6,350   555. 9,000

556. 3,859   557. 1,776   558. 8,025.4   559. 5,450   560. 9,900

561. 6,000   562. 7,349.9   563. 7,000   564. 1,000   565. 5,000

566. 4,116   567. 1,710   568. 2,000   569. 8,840   570. 1,950

571. 9,375.6   572. 8,560   573. 8,289   574. 4,900   575. 2,100

576. 5,400   577. 6,000   578. 8,164   579. 4,399   580. 6,430

581. 7,000   582. 8,610   583. 7,000   584. 8,450   585. 8,077.9

586. 8,380.9   587. 5,358   588. 3,288.9   589. 4,170.1   590. 1,400